T0193706

MONEY MOVE$

This is not a get-rich-quick scheme!
It's a conversation about money.

THERESA YONG

BALBOA.PRESS

A DIVISION OF HAY HOUSE

Balboa Press books may be ordered through booksellers or by contacting:

Balboa Press
A Division of Hay House
1663 Liberty Drive
Bloomington, IN 47403
www.balboapress.com
844-682-1282

Print information available on the last page.

Interior Image Credit: Mark Garvin

ISBN: 979-8-7652-2632-2 (sc)
ISBN: 979-8-7652-2634-6 (hc)
ISBN: 979-8-7652-2633-9 (e)

Library of Congress Control Number: 2022905292

Balboa Press rev. date: 06/03/2022

For Cait and Loli – my supernovas

CONTENTS

DISCLAIMER

Money Moves is not intended to treat, prevent, or cure any illness. Excessive spending, revolving debt, and poor saving habits may be symptoms of a serious condition. If you have any of these symptoms, you should consider consulting a professional (perhaps a shrink) if problems persist or worsen after reading this book. *Money Moves* has not been approved or endorsed by the SEC, NASD, NCAA, NAACP, NOW, HRC, or NAFTA or by any other organizations that don't presently come to mind.

Also, I should mention here that the big company I work for requires me to add some disclosures when I talk about certain financial vehicles and investments. Their presence is not meant to alarm you, only to satisfy my compliance department so I can keep the job I love so dearly!

It took me seven years (!!) to write this and although I have combed through and updated the facts and figures to reflect the most recent data, some of the numbers were still relevant and still have the desired effect, so I left them in. I don't know about you, but it just seems that the older I get, the faster the time goes!

INTRODUCTION

Where Do I Start?

Hi there. I'm Theresa Yong. My friends call me Tree. I have been dedicated to personal finance and retirement planning for the past twenty-one years during my career in the financial services industry. I've spent my time with large companies, giants in the insurance and retirement industries, and I have met face-to-face with more than ten thousand clients during that time. I'm pleased to have had the good fortune to meet and listen to thousands of hardworking people. Some of them have been well versed in personal finance, savvy with their money, and prepared for the future no matter what it may bring. However, for the majority, it pains me to say they often have little awareness and even worse preparation for building a sound money profile.

Through all these meetings, I believe I have come to know a reasonable random sampling of the US population, and the experience has inspired me to write *Money Moves*. You see, it's my firm belief that everyone is capable of managing money wisely. I also think that the country would be better off economically if everyone had a financial education. Therefore, it is my long-term intention to bring financial savvy to the US public education system.

Before I was off on my own meeting with everyday people, I studied. I went to Florida State University to become a physician, but soon found myself interested in business, finance, and entrepreneurship. I went on to earn my master of business administration from the University of Miami. I have always been fascinated by how money works, how to make some, how to make it work for me, and how to save it. After school, and while I was doing retirement consulting for a large company, I also opened and managed two start-up businesses in my free time. (Yes, I realize I may have a condition, but what can I say? I have a lot of energy. It's my thing.) With my incredible husband and the part-time help of my two school-aged daughters, we opened a successful restaurant in the Florida Keys. We were busy, yes, but it's nonstop excitement all the time around here. Go big or go home, I always say. We've since sold the restaurant, and I'm still with said large company, but I was promoted to assistant vice president, so la-ti-da!

Now that life is a bit simpler again, as I mentioned, it is my personal mission to change our education system so that basic personal finance is taught in school. It is important that we provide this information before we send our young adults out to face the wilds of the world. My hope is that by the time you reach the end of *Money Moves*, this will be your mission too! Perhaps that's wishful thinking, but a girl can dream.

So, with this brief overview of my life, which I'm giving so that you can get to know me, I want you to have an idea of what to expect in the following pages. *Money Moves* is intended to take the scariness out of money. My hope is to inspire you to be as excited as I am about saving, investing, and planning for retirement. Or maybe I will remain the only dork on the planet who actually really digs this stuff. But I don't think so. We all like to have money!

This guide is a simple resource for everyday people. It will help you understand that the headaches sometimes caused by personal financial matters can often be avoided or eliminated altogether with some basic practical steps. I'll follow with some translations and explanations of otherwise difficult terms that may seem to exist to deliberately confuse you about your own money. This, of course, is not the case. It's not rocket science, and I will prove it to you!

Let's Begin!
You: "Where do I start?"
Me: "How about at the beginning?"

When do we really need to start learning about money? The earlier, the better! You really can't start early enough, and conversely, it's never too late to start learning about *your own* money. No matter where you are in life, you will always face an unending barrage of financial decisions coming at you from all directions. Questions come at you every day of your life, such as the following:

- "What car should I buy? Or should I lease? Which is better?"
- "Where do I want to live?"
- "How much can I afford to spend on a house?"
- "What's better—owning or renting?"
- "How much does college cost?"
- "Can I afford to go?"
- "Will my kids be able to afford it?"
- "Is it even worth it?"
- "How will I pay these medical bills?"
- "How much does insurance cost?"
- "And what about vacation? When can I go, and how much can I spend?"
- "How will I ever retire?"
- "What is a 401(k)?"
- "What is an IRA?"
- "Do I need a ROTH? What is that?"

The more you learn and eventually come to know firsthand, the better off you will be at making decisions with your money and avoiding mistakes the next time an opportunity or challenge arises. It's in your best interests to be informed no matter what—that is a no-brainer. But how do you take confusion and convert it to competence and even confidence? You keep it simple.

Think back to when you first learned that money was a thing. When you're a kid, you rely solely on your parents and family to plant those tiny little seeds of understanding about money. Did you have an allowance or receive a few dollars for your birthday? Did you do chores for cash? Remember how exciting it was to have dollars in your pocket to buy something all on your own for the first time? You pick up little hints here and there, watching your parents spend and struggle, although you likely have no idea what you're witnessing. It's funny how you remember things that seemed insignificant at the time, but then later on you realize how profoundly influential they were on your method of "adulting."

I remember my first savings account. My mother opened it for me when I was five, no doubt at the urging of my grandfather who was a World War II veteran and a child of the Depression era. When I was a kid, going to the bank was as big of a deal as going to the playground at the local fast-food joint. It didn't happen very often, but when it did, it was going to be a good time!

That's because for every holiday, birthday, and little occasion, my parents and grandparents would give me some money to put into my savings account. After every deposit, my mother would show me how to enter the amount into my log and add it to the prior balance. It was exciting to see the money accumulate! Well, as exciting as it can be for a seven-year-old at a bank. Honestly, for the first couple of years I went without a fuss only because of the promise of a lollipop. Yes, it was back when people still carried around ledgers and wrote their deposits and withdrawals with an actual pen by hand. Of course, it was also in the 1980s when the interest rates were a bit more favorable for bank deposits. Those days are long gone.

It's amazing how readily I can recall going to the bank

(getting my lollipop) and watching my little bits of money add up. Of course, I didn't realize it at the time, but it made an impact on me and changed my understanding of money for the rest of my life. I will forever remember how important it is to save something of everything you make for yourself. That was the first lesson of my early financial education. I was lucky I had parents and grandparents who felt it was important to teach me the value of a dollar and who fostered my education about money and saving at an early age. What would have happened if my parents just hadn't had time for that? What if my family never really discussed money, its importance, and its ability to make or break my quality of life? Or worse, what if my parents were actually doing the opposite and modeling bad money habits for me? Where would I be now? I would be 100 percent reliant on the information I got at school or from the larger community. And that is where most people find themselves today.

Whether you had an experience like mine or not, it is never too late to revisit your priorities and set the right frame of mind for good money habits. Your tomorrow self will need it someday, and someday always comes sooner than you think.

Poor financial education is not necessarily the fault of our parents or the parents who raised them. I believe it is a failure on the part of our education system to equip young people with the basic tools they need to effectively manage and invest their hard-earned money. I have yet to see a comprehensive mandatory class on personal finance implemented in elementary, middle, or even high school in the current United States educational system. I have heard there are some states that are beginning to require this, but in Florida and Massachusetts, where I did all my primary and secondary schooling, passing a course in personal finance was never a prerequisite for graduation.

I have seen some experiments in partnership with elementary schools in tiny pockets across the United States. When my daughter was in elementary school, until about second grade, her school had an agreement with a local bank to install a "kids' branch" right on school property. It was housed in a restored train caboose and designated Twiglet Bank. Every Friday the kids would have the opportunity to make deposits and withdrawals. Their classmates served as tellers, under the supervision of actual bank staff. It was a wonderful idea and a great experience for all the kids who took part! We should definitely foster these types of relationships and learning opportunities for children, but in a fundamental rather than extracurricular way.

Your parents were likely never taught personal finance formally either, and thus relied on their parents for an education about the virtues of hard work and concentrated savings. It's like the telephone game, but across generations instead of individuals in a circle. It's no wonder that the vast majority of the American working class is terrified of the economy or the stock market. To add insult to injury, your parents, like mine, grew up in a time when money just wasn't discussed.

Few talked about how much they made or how to cover bills, pay mortgages, and buy things—especially not with their kids. Oftentimes this entire critical education was boiled down to little dictums such as "A penny saved is a penny earned" and "Not until Friday—payday." As a child, you would simply ask for stuff, and sometimes your parents would say yes, but mostly they would say no. And likely with good reason. They weren't just being mean. They were managing a budget, much to your surprise. Whatever your money experiences, habits—good or bad—or influences were, you have the ability to change and redefine how you want to structure your money life now.

Think back to your earliest money-managing lessons. What were they? Did your parents have money mantras—things they said over and over again when you were a kid? One I remember is "Money doesn't grow on trees!" Write down whatever memories come to mind and you'll have an idea of the foundation of your financial belief system. As you can imagine, this foundation will need to be either reinforced or reconstructed. If nothing else, it'll be good to know just where you are.

I remember being sixteen and itching to get my first real job. At that age, you haven't the first clue about what you should be doing, but you know you want to get out there and make money—your *own* money. My first job was at Dairy Queen making $4.50 an hour, which at the time was above the $4.25-per-hour minimum wage, so I thought I was doing pretty well. I was proud to have a job, and I couldn't wait to get my first paycheck.

As a teenager, you get to spend your money on fun stuff while your parents typically cover basic necessities. It is certainly nice to be able to spend someone else's money for food, water, and shelter and to reserve your own money for wants rather than needs. Parents love their kids so much that they happily provide these things. This is where I think the first lesson in fiscal responsibility would fit in nicely. Instead of quietly managing, parents have an excellent opportunity to introduce the concepts of banking, budgeting, and saving to their young worker bees. And as with anything in life, when you really want to learn something, start teaching it!

The earlier a child becomes comfortable with terms such as *bills, credit, budget, retirement, savings,* and *investments,* the better equipped they will be to face all the challenges and opportunities that enter the financial world every day— especially the avalanche of issues that come when applying for and attending college or any postsecondary training. Furthermore, the conversations will likely help the parent rein in family spending, which may be on a wayward path.

As you make your way through *Money Moves,* and if you have kids, sit down and talk with them about what it costs to run your life. Having meaningful, age-appropriate conversations about money will improve your financial life and set your kids up for success with their own financial lives. The more comfortable you are talking about money, the more confidence you will gain in managing money. Being open and honest about money with your dependents can also ease some of the money tension that inevitably builds up over time. Sharing that burden helps to alleviate it. As the old adage goes, "sunlight is the best disinfectant." Shedding light can help you find a solution to a challenge. You don't have to use actual numbers and figures, but you can easily show your kids how much cell phones, internet service, cable TV, and car insurance cost every month. Let them know that although they may not be responsible for paying for these things now, someday they will have to pay for these luxuries—because that's part of being grown up.

Going through your expenses is a great exercise that will set you up for success. It will also teach your kids the cost of adult life. It's a way to check and recheck where your money goes and where you may need to redirect it. I call these seemingly necessary expenses luxuries because all we really need in life is food, water, air, shelter, and some means of transportation. Your own car, cable TV service, and cell phone are certainly negotiable items on the needs vs. wants list, and the costs for these things vary widely. You can relate these costs to actual necessities such as rent or mortgage, food, utilities, and transportation to and from work. Then you can prioritize where you actually want your money to go and cut out the rest of the expenditures. That gives you instant savings!

Your family will begin to see that what they have become accustomed to may or may not be the bare essentials and that those costs may need to be negotiated once your children are out living on their own. Your children need to know that although it is nice to have a thousand-dollar iPhone X, it certainly isn't a necessity. In fact, a cell phone is not a necessity at all. People really do still have these strange things in their homes called landlines. It wasn't all that long ago that cell phones were the exception rather than the rule, and the internet was something you could use at the library or on occasion at home when you had the time to sit and wait for the dial-up. Okay, I can see that I am dating myself now, but I think you get the point.

Money may not seem like an easy subject to discuss and

understand, but I assure you that it can be. Often what makes it frustrating is a foundation of beliefs that inform decisions that don't serve you and you're not completely understanding how to make your money grow. You are taking steps now to solve these issues. And it is a little like learning a new language. There are fancy words and acronyms that further complicate the lingo. And then there's the subject of math. Although some math is inevitably involved, it is pretty simple stuff with a fascinating and important detail: it actually affects your quality of life.

In short, being open and honest about money is important for a healthy financial life, both for you and your family.

Wealthy people don't become wealthy by being perfect with their money. They just take calculated and educated risks. They have good savings habits and even better spending habits. *You don't build wealth by spending money faster than you can earn it.* That brings me to the #1 cardinal rule of money:

Live within Your Means

In other words, the money going out should be less than the money coming in. If you get nothing else out of this entire book (and I do hope that does not end up being the case), remember this rule. I am going to shove it in every spot throughout to remind you—don't worry. It's the golden rule of money, the one money commandment, the Holy Grail. If you get it, apply it, and remember it always, then *you will grow wealth.*

Obviously, being proficient with your money also makes it easier to provide the life you want for yourself and your loved ones. Everyone wants to be rich, but I think it's better said like this:

"Everyone wants to be rich enough."

But what is enough? Well, that is entirely up to you and

dependent on the life you want to lead. These are the decisions that you get to make. What is enough for you will depend on your ability and desire to work, to earn, and to use your earned money to make money for itself. And truth be told, there is a freedom that comes with simple living that can hardly be found elsewhere. For some, enough will be a camper overlooking the mountains with a trusted dog by their side. For others, it's a nice home with a great yard and a family. For others still, it will be a penthouse in New York City with private jets to Monaco and helicoptering to their local golf club. Whatever your enough looks like, you need financial savvy to reach that place and stay there—and I intend to give that savvy to you with *Money Moves*.

My vision is to raise the financial literacy of the people in our country and across the world, one person at a time. When everyone is comfortable with money, everyone wins. Consumer confidence is the engine of our economy, and each of us is the consumer. Each of us has an important role to play. We have to start at home and get our individual financial houses in order. The greatest news is that we each get to choose what is important to us.

You will follow a basic fundamental plan to stabilize your finances. The rest will be up to you! You'll have the room to make a lot of personal choices for living your best life. Let's take the first step together now, shall we? Read on, my friend! There's good stuff here!

How Does Money Make You Feel? (I'm Not Your Psychiatrist, I'm Your Financial Adviser!)

S eriously, though, when you think about money, how does it make you feel? Are you excited about it? anxious? nervous? ashamed? worried? under control? out of control? Does it instantly stress you out, or do you feel that you have a good handle on your money? All those feelings are perfectly acceptable, and they're all normal responses to money.

The following is from the American Psychological Association's 2016 *Stress in America* report:

> Money, work and the economy continue to be the most frequently cited causes of stress for Americans, as they have every year for the past 5 years. In addition, a growing number of Americans are citing personal health and their family's health as a source of stress.

> Significant sources of stress include money (75 percent), work (70 percent), the economy (67 percent), relationships (58 percent), family responsibilities (57 percent), family health problems (53 percent), personal health concerns

(53 percent), job stability (49 percent), housing costs (49 percent) and personal safety (32 percent).[1]

I know I don't need to tell you, as by now it's common knowledge, that money is a significant burden on the lives of most Americans. I imagine it's a significant burden on the lives of most humans. "Money makes the world go 'round" as the old saying goes. Managing money can be stressful, but it does not have to be. It is all within your control; you just have to grab hold of it and whip it into shape.

The first step to getting a hold of your money is to honestly assess how you naturally interact with it. You must be 100 percent honest with yourself, or else this whole journey of learning and acquiring financial acumen simply will not produce results. It does you no good if you kid yourself about how you're doing financially. When your credit card bills come in every month, do you open them right away or let them sit there for a while? Do they make you anxious? Do you tend to pay bills on time, or do you often pay late fees? Do you dream of being debt-free, or do you believe you will always have debts? Your answers to these questions serve as a barometer of your basic comfort level with money. I want to make you completely comfortable and confident with your money, but we have to find your starting mark.

Here's a good way to start: Take three deep breaths. Clear your mind of any preconceived notions of where you think you should be in life. Now just state the facts. Try to catch yourself if you say something that seems to be the "right" answer but is not what you actually do with your money. No one wants to admit if they're doing something wrong, but you're only talking with yourself. Don't compare yourself to others, to society, or to conventional wisdom. You know the truth anyway.

---

[1] American Psychological Association, *Stress in America*, 2016, http://ar2016.apa.org/stress-in-america/.

Now try this: say one thing out loud that is true about yourself and your reaction to money. To make you feel more at ease, I'll go first:

I have a hard time keeping cash in my pocket. It seems to either burn a hole or vanish without my knowing (or, more likely, willfully refusing to acknowledge) it.

That wasn't so hard for me as I have been doing this sort of thing for years now, but the first time I had to say it to myself, it was as if I was saying to myself, *you can't be trusted with your own cash on your person at any time.*

That's a scary thing to say to oneself. It was seeming to say that I couldn't be trusted with my own money! That's not necessarily what the statement is saying, though. From another perspective, it means that I need to be more conscious of how much I spend when I carry cash. So, with this newfound self-realization, I can change my behavior. Now, I typically don't carry cash because it's difficult for me to keep track of it. Instead, I give myself an allotted amount that I can afford for the day and I refrain from spending more than that. This new framework prevents me from buying things I don't need just because I have cash on me.

This kind of self-discipline is particularly important for those of us who are paid for our work in cash. When I was waiting tables, I went through a great deal of cash in a week, and at times I ended up being short on my bills because of this bad habit. I then decided that I needed to deposit my money into the bank as soon after my shift as possible so I wouldn't blow it. And not carrying too much cash saves me from having to buy a bigger house to store all that unneeded stuff, so that's a bonus!

As a result of this realization, I practice a few habits that help me keep better track of my money. I almost always use my debit card at point-of-sale (where the card doesn't leave my sight) businesses. That way I have a written record of where my money goes. Then I begrudgingly check my expenditures on a daily, weekly, and sometimes monthly basis to see what I am spending my money on. Second, I have a threshold amount under which I will not use my debit card (because it's a waste to whip out a card for a tiny purchase). This keeps me from buying many needless low-cost items. Those little items seem small as a onetime purchase, but they add up quickly when you buy them frequently (think Starbucks). Stopping myself from making these types of purchases saves me money, particularly at the grocery store, the gas station, and convenience stores. I try not to even enter a gas station convenience store if I can help it; it's too tempting to buy a quick water or a snack. For the amount of time that I spend driving, I know it will put a significant dent in my budget if I give in to that urge.

Okay, so it's your turn. Go ahead, say something true about yourself and money that you have never said aloud or admitted to yourself before. It might be something positive or something that you find challenging about money. If it's positive, you likely don't give yourself enough credit for being fiscally responsible or doing the right thing. Good habits, even small ones, can add to your bottom line quickly (and with surprising results).

I'll give you another one of mine to help you out, this time a positive truth.

"I am always thinking about the future, and so I plan accordingly."

That doesn't mean I don't live for today. I do. I try to take pleasure in the little moments of every day because that is what life is truly about. However, I am also aware that statistics dictate that I am likely to live a very long time, and in that time, I will have many obligations. I have always been a planner, even when I was a young child. I look forward to payday so I can pay myself first (my #1 obligation) through my retirement plan, and I also look forward to paying my bills and meeting my other important obligations. This is a practice that I find both rewarding and validating. As soon as my bills are paid, I feel instant relief. I know that may sound weird, and it may not be true for you, which is totally okay. You just have to make sure that you can meet your obligations every month without feeling as if you are just treading water or barely keeping afloat. No one can feel at ease and in control of their finances if they feel as if they're always drowning.

Does facing how money makes you feel surprise you? Be clear with yourself about your feelings and natural inclinations so you will know your starting line on this financial journey. Can you see the path ahead? Can you envision a life of financial freedom? Remember, "A journey of a thousand miles begins with a single step" (Lao-tzu).

Let's Talk about Money. No, Really, We Need to Talk

Now that I have you thinking about how you feel about money and how you alone react to it (because everyone is different), let's talk about what purpose money serves in your life. The foregoing exercise was meant to get your gears turning to think about how you handle and utilize your money.

The purpose money serves in life is defined by your *why*: why do you need it, why do you want it, and why do you expend your precious time and energy to accumulate it? Every person's individual why may be different, but there are some universal truths to why we, as Americans, work for and want money. Here are a few of them:

- "I work for money so that I can provide for myself and my family."
- "I want money so that I don't have to worry about anyone having to take care of me."
- "I save money so that I can have a comfortable retirement."
- "I earn money so that I can buy or rent a safe place to live."
- "I work so that I can afford nice things."

- "I invest so that I won't have to work until I drop dead."
- "I save money so that I can travel."

The list of why anyone works for money is endless and unique to each individual. We are willing to give up time, energy, talent, and resources to accumulate money, not to mention that we *must* do this in order to survive. Each reason for surviving *and thriving* is as good as the next. It's how we utilize the money once we get it that defines how effective or successful we are at attaining the purpose (the why) that we set out to achieve.

For our efforts to be validated, we have to first recognize what we are trying to achieve. Then we must set realistic, periodic goals to get there. Building wealth and becoming financially independent is the result of discipline applied to calculated, sometimes monotonous, daily habits. That may not sound like the most exciting of pursuits, but it is in no way beyond your control. Once you begin to see the numbers growing in your accounts, you will gain a new sense of confidence in your financial life. And you will be on a whole new money life trajectory. It doesn't even take that long to get on this more gratifying and validating course. But it does take clarity and commitment. The problem is, most people equate wealth and a comfortable lifestyle with some mysterious stroke of luck that is achievable by only a very few. This could not be farther from the truth.

I can't tell you how many times I have heard, when I've asked my clients how they plan to retire, the response "I'm going to win the lottery," followed by a sort of sad, awkward chuckle. I may not say it out loud, and you will not see my disdain for this flippant response, but I hate that reply, as does any financial professional worth her salt. I'm literally biting my tongue and rolling my eyes back in my head, and my ears are folding in on themselves, when I hear that. Know this: there is a reason the lottery is called "the poor man's tax."

Don't get me wrong, playing the lottery is not inherently wrong and not without its thrills. The sheer daydream of imagining this incredible stroke of luck and the effects it could have on your life is entertainment enough to merit spending a dollar or two. *But* understand that that is exactly what it is: entertainment. The lottery is not a financial plan for your future. It is not even remotely what you would call an investment. What it is, is a gamble—a remote, minuscule, minute cosmic improbability that is won by less than 0.001 percent of the population. To put this into perspective, there are very few people who have won jackpots greater than one million dollars since the inception of the first US lottery in Puerto Rico in 1964. The number of millionaires made in California between 1985 when it started until 2019 is two hundred seventy-four. That's about eleven per year in one of the most populated states in the country. In California, where the population is forty million, the chance of becoming a millionaire through the state lottery is 0.000029 percent! That is a tiny number to hang your future on. And, of course, it's not reality. It's not even a wing and a prayer!

Now I know clients are trying their best to make light of what can sometimes feel like a daunting situation when they say stuff like that. But for those of you who make this statement to a financial professional, know that it says many other things about you and your money life, besides the fact that you have no plan. For one, it further exemplifies your discomfort with all things financial. It's like saying, "Oh, retirement? Yeah, I'm just going to wing it" or "I'm not going to live that long anyway." These responses are an attempt to deflect attention away from feelings of helplessness. They are simply cries for help. If you truly think that you're going to "wing it" for retirement, or if you hope to win the lotto, then you really are at a point where you feel hopeless. You may even believe that you're never going to retire, and that is not good.

The good news is that this frame of mind stops now. The effort it takes to put small actions into place to turn your money life around is no greater than the effort it takes to live in fear and worry over a financial life that is out of control. So, spend your energy where it counts!

You are taking control of your financial future now. You are capable of making sound and profitable financial decisions. You are perfectly able to understand your own finances, your money, and how you will grow it. There is no wrong way to save money. Yes, some ways are more efficient, more practical, and more advantageous, but *when you save money, you are doing something right*. Because of our unique experiences, likes, dislikes, and priorities, the way you save will be different from the way I save. The important thing to strive for is the achievement of your why, the goals that are important to you, whatever those may be.

Your Money Personality

In my many years as a financial consultant, I have heard more excuses, awkward comments, uncomfortable silences, and strange, self-deprecating anecdotes than I could ever write down. Wherever you are on your financial journey, it's okay. You will be fine. You can learn this stuff. It's not rocket science (I've said that before!). In fact, when you break it down and understand the terminology and know what questions to ask, it can be quite liberating to know that, yes, you too can handle your own money and do it well.

The first thing you have to do is to ask yourself, "What is my money personality?" To answer that question, you need to understand what a money personality is.

A money personality is your innate tendency to either spend or save money. For some, saving money is like brushing their teeth—part of a daily routine. It's natural and feels good. For others, saving money is like going to the dentist. They do it only begrudgingly and, shall we say, less than enthusiastically. And these savers frequently dip into the pot. Farther down on the spending spectrum are those who arrange their lives so that income is insufficient before it even comes in. Practices such as overextending on rent, car payments, and nonessentials such as cable and fancy phones may make you feel good outwardly, but inwardly, and in your bank account, they cause major stress. Still others buy things because they believe that money only has value when it is exchanged for something. Social scientists call this type of spending "conspicuous consumption." At first, the person gets a rush from this spending, but as with other bad habits, this rush is short-lived and leaves one with a nasty headache.

Do you like to spend money? Do you like to save money? Do you spend cash (like me) as if there's a hole in your pocket? Do you hoard whatever you can and hardly spend at all? Do you get queasy at the mention of the word *investment*? Do you enjoy paying bills? Are you chronically late paying off your debts? Do you want to live large, or do you prefer simpler, smaller living? Do you tend to live in the moment with your money, or do you like to save for a rainy day? Do you live paycheck to paycheck, or do you have enough money to make it through a temporary illness or job loss?

Your answers to these questions can help you assess how you are with your money. They can help you get a firm grasp on the habits you are already nurturing to reach your financial goals and on those that you can work on to change or control if you find yourself completely off track.

I enjoy saving. I also enjoy spending. I would say that my money personality is more in line with a balanced approach. When my saving is out of balance, I can immediately feel it. When my spending is out of balance, I can feel that too, often more so. For instance, periodically, let's say once or twice a year, I find myself going out on a particular day and just doing whatever it is that comes to mind. I call it a me-day. I'll go out in the morning, get my hair done, perhaps get a massage, go out to lunch, and then head to a few stores or a mall and buy whatever I feel I may need or want at that moment. It adds up. I don't restrict myself (but I don't pay full retail either), and I usually end up buying a few suits or outfits for work, a trinket or two, and something for my family. If I did that more often than a few times a year, it would put the hurt on my budget and my overall financial plan, so I keep this behavior in check. I do enjoy it, but I am not what you would call a shopaholic. I don't enjoy shopping that much (I do spend my money in other ways), but once in a while I do like to buy pretty things. I used to feel guilty about it the next day. I would think about what my husband would say and figure out some justification for my spending, as if I had done something wrong. I have come to understand that it is not wrong to purchase what I want or need as long as I can afford it. I've since learned to adjust my budget and my finances so as to accommodate these excursions a few times a year.

Everyone has their thing, whether it's a collection of some sort, a hobby, or a love for travel. You are allowed to spend your hard-earned money. *Money Moves* is not going to try to convince you to stop spending altogether. The goal is to *live within your means* and adjust your expectations to match your income so that you can live comfortably. Living comfortably includes spending some money on the things you enjoy while being conscious about your long-term goals and obligations.

You've heard of those who love to spend money on just about anything—the spendthrifts. You've likely heard of those who thrive on saving every last dime they can—the misers. I say that there exists a whole spectrum of money personalities between the traditional miser and spendthrift. I think people tend to lean more toward one or the other, but if you have even a small sense of fiscal responsibility within you, you can realign yourself when you know you've gone too far toward one extreme or the other. Being good with your money is a give-and-take; it's about awareness. It is a delicate balancing act to live between instant gratification and depriving yourself of everything you want. It's called quality of life, and it's optimized when you balance your needs against your wants and keep them all in line with your cash flow.

The point is, people rarely take a look at where they are on the spectrum. When you take notice and realize where you are, you can become better prepared to anticipate when an occasion to overdo things will arise. If you recognize that such a spree is coming, then you can prepare to keep it in financial check. You may spend, but knowing that you will be spending, you can adjust your savings soon after. Knowing that you are or will be saving may encourage you to go ahead and spend some money on something that will improve your quality of life. It's achieving a balance between the two—gratification and deprivation—that will keep you comfortable and ultimately make you happy. No one can be happy saving every little penny and never enjoying life. Alternatively, no one can be happy spending everything they have and then worrying about meeting all their monthly obligations or paying for a comfortable retirement.

Sometimes you need to tell yourself, "No, I don't need that right now." You'd be surprised how much more satisfying a purchase can be when you know you worked hard and sacrificed to save for it and eventually reached your goal, instead of putting it on a credit card, oftentimes paying much more than the sales price because of the interest charges. Instant gratification isn't all it's cracked up to be. It's a bit of a false promise. Have you ever experienced the letdown of wanting something, charging it, acquiring it, and later realizing it wasn't that great? Then you spot something else you want, something "better", and before you know it, you've moved on to the next thing. It can be a vicious cycle. Nip the instant gratification cycle in the bud and break out your budget. You'll thank yourself later when you are free from the chains of credit card debt. We'll talk more about that type of indentured servitude soon enough.

Give yourself some time to really become aware of all your current habits, feelings, and beliefs related to money. Next, we are going to delve into the money nitty-gritty.

What Is the Lingo?

Now that I have you thinking about yourself and your attitude toward money, your purposes for your money, and your money personality, let's talk briefly about some of the common terms and definitions you will need to know. These are words and phrases that will come up frequently, so you should get comfortable with them. They're just part of the money vernacular, including questions such as "What is and what is not an investment?" "What's an asset?," and "What's a liability?" You should commit these terms to memory. I'll reference them frequently throughout *Money Moves*, so it is important that you understand their meanings, as follows:

- **Asset**—something of value that you own and that can be exchanged for money.
- **Liability**—something you owe.
- **Commodity**—raw material in limited quantity (e.g., cotton, grain, precious metal); a product of use, advantage, or value.
- **Dividend**—your share in investment return as an owner; anything received as a bonus, as a reward, or in addition to or beyond what is expected. Essentially, this is your return on investment without having to sell the asset.

Now let's talk briefly about what an **investment** is and what it isn't. I'll elaborate on investments frequently in *Money Moves*, so it is important to provide my definition of an investment. In order to build wealth, you must have a firm grasp of this concept too.

investment (*n*): the action or process of investing
money for profit or material result.

This statement is true, but the definition is by no means complete. You are making an investment of time, energy, and effort to read and process *Money Moves*. You may have even made an investment of some money to purchase it. My definition of *investment* has two parts: (1) anyplace you put money where you expect it to grow; (2) any allocation of time, effort, energy, or attention from which you expect a benefit or positive effect on your quality of life.

I don't think the word *investment* should be limited to a monetary meaning. To illustrate my meaning, I'll give an example: When you take classes to improve your skills or your competency, you are investing both money, which is a precious asset, and time—a more precious and fleeting commodity. Money is undoubtedly an important and valuable asset; everyone knows this. However, time is finite. You have only so much time in a day, a week, a month, a year, and in fact, your life. That makes your time your most precious asset. You will never have more time. You will never be able to buy more time. You will only be able to maximize the time you have.

Many people believe that time is expendable. There is a fatal error in this type of thinking, pun intended. I want to challenge your ideas about time as it relates to value, life, and money. Time is money. Time is value. Time is life. You might have heard all the world's most renowned investors and famous billionaires utter these very same words. You have likely heard the most influential teachers, gurus, and spiritual leaders say the same thing. I will tell you, they are all absolutely right. You are either gaining or losing with your time, and it's all in how you choose to spend each moment of it.

So, let's take this time to make the most sense of money matters. I am truly honored by the investment of your time. I will do my best to make it pay dividends. I want you to think differently about what an investment truly is. And as I describe different investments throughout *Money Moves*, I want you to think holistically about how you can apply this information to your life so as to make it better.

Budgeting—Yes, It's Necessary

can just hear you complaining about budgeting, like a little kid asking if he really must brush his teeth. I know, I know, doing a budget sucks, but it's very necessary. You really only need one solid template, and then you won't have to do it again for a long while. So, quit your whining and get out your bank statements and a nice glass of Malbec, cuz you're going to need it to take the edge off.

Clear your dining room table or your desk. Get out your bank statements from the last six months. Then get out your credit card statements from the last two to four months and set them aside for now. Gather a legal pad or a notebook (or an Excel spreadsheet if that's your thing) that you can go back to and make notes in later. Then start categorizing where your money goes every month. Write down what you spend your money on. Every. Last. Bit. Of. It.

Following are some common accounting/budget categories (of course, you may use whichever terms make the most sense to you):

- Housing
  Rent, mortgage, homeowners association fees, etc.

- Transportation
  Cars, gasoline, public transit, parking, etc.

- Food
  Groceries, lunches, small personal meals out, snacks, etc.

- Entertainment
  Social meals, gatherings, restaurants, bars, leisure activities, movies, etc.

- Clothing
  Personal clothing (not work related).

- Work-related expenses
  Clothes, uniforms, office supplies, work tools, etc.

- Utilities
  Electric, water, sewer, heat, cable, internet, phone, etc.

- Insurance
  Homeowners or renters, property, car, luxury, life, health, etc.

- Medical
  Expenses not covered by insurance.

- Travel
  Any personal/pleasure travel.

- Shopping
  Nonessential items.

- Repairs and maintenance
  For appliances or large assets such as cars; landscaping; pool cleaning.

- Loans
  Any personal loans not related to another category.

- Education
  School-related expenses for yourself or your dependents.

- Luxury purchases
  Hobby-related or nonessential expenses such as for boating, sports, or other interests.

- Credit
  Short-term credit payments, that is, credit cards, not mortgages.

- Pets
  Any pet-related expenses, including pet insurance and boarding.

- Miscellaneous
  Whatever doesn't fit into any of the other categories.

This list is not exhaustive, and you may use any category that relates more to your personal situation, as long as you understand what goes into that category and the purchases you make are easily traceable.

Once you have categorized all your expenses from your bank statements for the prior six months, add up the total expense for each category. Take that number and divide it by six to get your average monthly expenses for that category (you have six bank statements in front of you, not twelve, so you'll divide by six). Take special note of where the largest portions of your money are being spent each month. Then take all your categories and separate them into two main piles, if you will: essential and nonessential. I like to think of these as negotiable and nonnegotiable, respectively. In truth, everything is negotiable. You have to do quite a reality check before you realize what is truly negotiable. But we will stick with *essential* and *nonessential* because it helps to take the emotion out of the analysis, at least for now. You only separate these two types of expenses from one another so that you can get a better idea of the areas where you can make cuts if times get tough or if you have a specific savings goal and it is truly a priority to find the money to save when you don't currently have it.

A few examples of essential expenses are as follows:

- Housing (You've gotta live somewhere!)
- Transportation (You've gotta get to work!)
- Food (You've gotta eat!)
- Insurance (You should protect your assets [or ass for that matter, in the case of health insurance]!)

A few examples of nonessential expenses are as follows:

- Cable
- Shopping
- Entertainment
- Travel
- Hair, nails, spa, golf club, beer club
- Landscaper or pool cleaner service
- Gym
- Massage
- Luxury upgrades

These are only examples; these lists are not the definitive sources for essential and nonessential expenses. A good rule of thumb to remember, however, is that to survive, at the minimum we need food, water, air, clothing, and shelter. Those are the most basic necessities in life. All else can be considered a matter of preference, how you like to live your life. You will survive without cable. We did it not so long ago. I know, the horror!

Everyone has to have something to do—a hobby, a passion, a pastime. You just have to categorize those things as nonessential because you do not need those things to live, breathe, eat, or earn your keep, so they are technically not necessary. Later, when you analyze how much you are bringing in and compare it to how much is going out, you can evaluate and negotiate with yourself (and/or your significant other) as to the importance of said nonessential expenses in your budget.

If you have negative cash flow continually from month to month, you are soon going to be in a hole deeper than you are able to get out of. That will lead you straight to financial ruin. And since you are reading *Money Moves*, I am guessing that this is not the direction you intend to be heading. The budgeting and the evaluation of your financial snapshot—your fiscal picture at this point in time—is the hardest part of the whole financial planning process. It requires some real soul-searching and self-reflection, both for you and your significant other if you have one. To get on the right path, you have to cut the fat. You have to trim and reduce where you can, readjust, and put your money to work for you. After the initial budgeting is done, the rest will usually fall into place little by little. Plus, the rest is a lot more fun!

Why Bother Budgeting?

How can you know where to go if you don't know where you are? To find out where you are is as simple as marking your starting point on a map. Try doing that if you have no clue where you are. Pretty difficult to figure out which path to take toward your destination, isn't it?

Now imagine you're staring at a dartboard. The middle is your goal, of course. But then the lights go out. How are you going to hit the middle now? Are you going to just start throwing darts in the dark and hope for the best? I assure you, when the lights come back on, you will not be surprised at the result. You'll likely have hit the wall, the lamp, maybe a part of the board, and maybe even your best buddy sitting next to you quietly sipping his beer, who now has a dart sticking out of his forehead, unfazed because of his buzz.

The budgeting part of this whole financial planning business is as essential as having the lights on when you throw darts. Unfortunately, far too many people are flinging darts in the dark, hoping they will hit the middle at least once. It doesn't happen often, and when it does do so by pure luck, continuing to hit the target gets more and more unlikely.

In financial terms, it is better to hit close to the middle almost every time over your lifetime (at the very least, get the dart on the board) than to throw several darts and only hit the middle once or, worse, never hit it at all. Do you want to know the big secret to this analogy? If you do hit closer and closer to the middle throughout your life, eventually you will hit the middle every time because you will be getting better and better at aiming for that goal. The ability to make good financial decisions again and again comes with practice, patience, and experience—just like throwing a great set of darts (or becoming excellent at any other sport, recreation, or game that you prefer. It's universally applicable).

Where Does All My Money Go?!

After you have sifted and sorted all your expenditures for the past six months from your bank accounts, you should grab those credit card statements I told you to set aside. Take a deep breath and a sip of wine and get ready. If you are like me and most of my clients (and most people in general), you will use a credit card on a weekly, if not a daily, basis. Credit cards are a necessary evil and can sometimes be an asset, but I am getting ahead of myself. We are going to go into much detail about this topic a little later.

I use a credit card for many of my everyday purchases. This may or may not be true for you. I tend to have a general rule about what I will or will not put on a credit card and what I will put on my debit card. It may be just a personal quirk, but I try to keep my debit card on me at all times. That means I do not hand my debit card to anyone who might walk away with it. Call me crazy, but since the money on my debit card comes right out of my bank account, I find it poses more risk to me directly if someone decides to attempt to defraud me with it. A credit card, on the other hand, has protections built in, not the least of which is that you usually don't pay the bill until the end of the billing cycle. This means I have a whole month to detect fraud, alert my credit card company to it, and dispute it before they can make me pay for any unauthorized purchases. That in and of itself is protection enough for me to use a credit card at places where the card may leave my sight (restaurants, bars, hotels, resorts, etc.). My logic is, the more I can hold on to my debit card or, better yet, input my PIN with it, the more protected my actual money will be.

Let's get back to the credit card statements. Take a look at them quickly. Are there several pages or just a few? If you have many pages, you may be using your credit card too much. If there are too few pages, you may be using it too little. Whichever is the case, look deeper now and start to discern where you tend to use credit. Do this for a month or two. Are there unusual purchases, or are the things you buy pretty standard? Do you have a separate gas card? Do you have many separate, specific purchase cards? How many cards do you have? More importantly, do you carry any balances on these cards over to the next month? Do you know the interest rate on each of your cards?

These questions may seem daunting, but the answers are vitally important to tracking down where your money goes each month. Now, just like with the bank statements, look at your credit card statements and categorize all your purchases (many credit card apps do this automatically for you and allow you to download the sorted report, saving you a bit of time!). Are there any overlaps with your bank statements? Do you sometimes use your debit card or pay cash for a purchase, but other times use a credit card for the same thing? Don't worry, this happens a lot. The problem with this habit is that if you carry a balance on a credit card, you are likely paying interest on that balance. That means that you are effectively paying more for the same item just by using your credit card to pay for it. That's right! When you use a credit card and you do not pay back the balance every month, you pay the credit card company for the convenience of using their money now, while you pay them back later.

In this interest rate environment, carrying a balance can often mean paying upward of 16 percent for even the most creditworthy borrowers. To put it into real dollar terms, if you have a running balance of $2,000 on a credit card with a 16 percent interest rate and you keep that balance for a year, you pay an extra $320 for the privilege of using the card now, rather than waiting until you actually have the money to buy the item(s). The interest can really add up. In 2015, the average American household had $15,706 in credit card balances. That's an extra $2,513 in interest charges on the lowest-interest-rate cards out there! Let's not even get into specific store cards and online retail cards, whose interest rates can run as high as 29 percent per year! That's an extra $209 per month of fees on average. Needless fees.

I remember my first credit card. I had just turned eighteen and had a job and was going to school, feeling pretty good about myself. I wanted to get my mother something special for her birthday, which was in May. She always loved emeralds, her birthstone. Because I was now an "adult", I told myself I could afford to buy her some jewelry, which she also loves. *After all, it is for Mom,* I thought. *She deserves it. She's done so much for me. And besides, I can just work harder to save and buy it.*

I went to the mall. I walked around looking in all the jewelry stores until I found a bracelet and a matching pair of earrings that I thought my mom would like. Not thinking of the price of real gold with real emeralds in it, I asked to look at them more closely. I don't recall the look on the salesperson's face when I asked, but I imagine it was something along the lines of humor or disdain, whichever. It was a dead Wednesday afternoon at the mall, and I guess he just needed something to do. I don't doubt for a minute that he knew I couldn't afford the pieces. He took them out slowly, describing the vibrancy of the color, the detail of the gold, the accent of the tiny diamonds. I wasn't really listening. I had already made up my mind to buy them. I said, "I'll take them," just like they do in the movies. Hah!

He said, perhaps a little shocked, "All right, that will be three hundred fifty dollars." I looked up quickly. I stammered. I opened my eyes wider. (Remember, this was twenty-five years ago.)

"Would you like it gift wrapped?" he asked.

"Uh, it's for my mom," I said, barely.

I thought quickly. I knew I didn't have that money. I thought quickly again. "Can I write a check?" I asked. This was going south fast. What would I do after that? How long would it take for that check to clear? What would happen if I didn't get the money in the account fast enough? I was getting paid again that Friday, so I went through all the possible scenarios. I knew writing bad checks is a major no-no. My brain scramble was all for naught.

"No, we don't accept personal checks. However, we do take credit cards. Do you have a Schmales charge?" he asked, quite amused at my inexperience, I'm sure.

Now I am not sure if back then the salespeople were making the kinds of commissions from pushing credit cards to young, inexperienced consumers with the promise of increased savings as much as salespeople are doing this today, but at that time I really didn't care. I saw a way out of a very embarrassing situation.

"I don't have one yet, but I am interested," I said, a wave of relief flushing across my brow.

"Well, great. If you sign up today, you get 10 percent off your purchase," he said with a half smile.

"Okay," I said. "What do I need to do?"

He presented me with a four-page form in fluent legalese that not only overwhelmed me but also basically asked for permission to get every piece of information available on me, except my blood type. And at the end, it basically asked me to sign my life away. Like Ariel in *The Little Mermaid*, I grabbed the pen, turned my head, closed my eyes, and signed on the dotted line. Back then, credit card companies were not required, as they are today, to put the interest rate that they charge you in big bold print right on the front, where it's easy to see what you are agreeing to. I had no idea what I was doing. Luckily, (or perhaps, unluckily) I was instantly approved (Surprise! "No credit history? No problem!") and walked away like a proud peacock with my perfect purchase. I was so excited to present it to my mom, I practically skipped like a fool the whole length of the mall toward my car.

Looking back, I don't see this as a bad experience or a bad decision to get that credit card. It was a series of mistakes and opportunities that presented themselves in such a way to persuade me to make a split-second decision that could have potentially affected my credit score and me for the rest of my life. I know that now. I did not know that then. I had no frame of reference. I was aware that credit cards had interest rates, but I didn't know how significant this fact was. I didn't even think to ask. When I got my first statement, I saw the interest rate printed in the upper right-hand corner. I was in total shock: 27.88 percent! I knew right then and there that I needed to pay off the balance as quickly as possible.

In that particular situation at the jewelry store, if I had known to calm down, check my ego, and ask the appropriate questions, I think I would have made a better decision. I would have asked if the bracelet and earrings were always in stock or if they were a special set. I would have inquired about having them held until the next week, when I knew I would have the money. I would have waited until I had the money in hand or in the bank to pay the credit card off immediately. I may have considered getting the card just for the discount and then paying the balance and canceling the card within the month.

If I were to walk into a store today and find that I couldn't afford something, I wouldn't hesitate to decline to buy it, without any remorse or embarrassment. I don't care what other people think of my ability to buy (or finance) something. They are not privy to or in charge of my bank account. I am. *You should never be embarrassed to say you won't purchase something or that you simply can't afford it.* No one is in charge of your financial success but you. You will never be financially free if you can't learn to say no to spending. No one ever got rich by spending their way there.

Furthermore, if I find myself in the middle of a high-pressure sales tactic, I quickly excuse myself and walk out. I am not a fan of pushy salespeople. It baffles me how they get anyone to buy anything that way. It's a huge red flag for me. If a salesperson is trying desperately to get you to buy something, then he or she is not telling you the whole story. There's something missing. Confident salespeople present the product, the material information, and the pros and the cons of the product, and give the buyer the time and space to consider a purchase. Truly good, honest salespeople never worry about making every sale because they know that their product may not be the best choice for every possible buyer. Good salespeople give the right information, are relaxed, and are sure of their competence. They believe in their products, and they help facilitate the sale to the right buyer. For buyers, that kind of trust is invaluable, and for sellers that kind of trust is priceless as it creates loyal customers for life and reliable repeat business.

The point of my story is that we all learn from our mistakes. We all make them. We have to. They are essential to our growth. The main thing is not to allow our mistakes to paralyze us and prevent us from making decisions in the future because of our fear of making more mistakes.

When you are looking at your credit card statements, your bank account statements, and now your budget, I want you to notice where the larger chunks of your money are going every month. Is your money being spent mainly on essential or nonessential items? Are you paying interest on your credit cards, car loans, or other types of loans? How high is the rate? Can you improve it? Are you paying yourself through saving? Where is your money going? Take a look; figure it out. Then ask yourself: "Am I happy with how I am spending my money? What do I have to show for all my hard work?"

If you are not completely happy, which I am sure you are not, then you need to make a change. Let's do this! Do you notice certain areas where a good chunk of your money is going and it surprises you? Perhaps it's your five-dollar-per-day coffee shop habit (like me), or the extra four dollars you spend at the convenience store each time you go to fill up your gas tank. Or maybe it's the fifty-dollar-per-night eating out at a restaurant each weekend that surprises you. Whatever it is, you and I both know we can find some area where you are spending more than you should or even want to spend. Doing a budget review or a financial checkup periodically is good for everyone, no matter how much they make or how little they may have. Everyone has room to adjust their budget and set aside money, slowly but surely, to reach those seemingly far-off goals. Even a drop of water every day will eventually fill a bucket.

Sometimes your incoming money is tight and you aren't spending for the obvious drains (that is, eating out at restaurants or getting coffee). Sometimes you need to do more analysis to make adjustments to what you are spending your money on. Could you shop around for less expensive insurance? Could you trade in your BMW for a Honda Civic? Could you cancel the cable or trade for a lower cost streaming service? Could you get a different cellular plan? Could you work out at the park or use an app instead of paying for a gym membership? Could you teach yourself the ukulele from YouTube rather than pay for lessons? Some of these examples are silly, but I am trying to illustrate that if it is a priority for you to find financial freedom sooner rather than later, then you have to change now. You have to change your spending habits, your savings habits, and likely your overall attitude toward the value of certain things as compared to the value of being financially independent. I know it's fun to drive a luxury car, live in a McMansion, and eat out every night, but if you can't afford to reach your financial goals and do all those things, then you can't afford those things. And that is perfectly okay.

I told you there would be a reality check. It will be a constant theme throughout *Money Moves*. Get used to it. I am trying to change what you think you know about money and turn it into what you really know about money. I also want to help you check your ego, because we Americans love to make money decisions based on what other people might think about us. We have to stop that, and that means putting our egos aside and doing the real behind-the-scenes work of building wealth. I promise you, nothing will make you feel more at ease or prouder of yourself than true financial independence. And no one else needs to know when you've achieved it!

To reinforce that point, here are a few interesting facts:

Did you know ...

... that nearly half of all new luxury car sales are leases?

That seems surprising, right? Because if you have the money for a new luxury car, why wouldn't you just buy it? A lot of people don't do things that way. The problem is, most people can't afford to buy a new luxury car outright, but they can come up with the down payment and monthly installments for a short-term lease. This could indicate that people are living beyond their means, right? Right and wrong. It could just mean that people are fickle when it comes to cars and they don't want to be tied down to one for the long haul. The average American changes cars, bought or leased, every four years. Despite our natural consumer tendencies even toward large purchases such as cars, both scenarios—leasing a luxury vehicle and getting a different car every four years—are bad for a good financial plan. Cars are depreciable, meaning that they lose value over time. They are not assets unless they become collectibles. With the availability of cars in the marketplace, it is quite difficult to make money off of appreciating classic cars. Plus, it takes a lot of patience, maintenance, storage, and overall TLC, so your investment is constant, and cars are not very liquid assets (they're difficult to turn into cash at a moment's notice). People in the classic car business are primarily there because of their love for classic cars. They may have a distant second motivation to make money off that love.

Sometimes we need to tell ourselves, "You do not need to live like the Joneses." I am not sure who the Joneses are, but I do know they're subliminal bullies, pushing their neighbors into crushing debt with their showy latest gadgets, coolest cars, and biggest houses. Don't play the comparison game; it is never in your best interests. This reminds me of a commercial I saw on TV a few years back: A guy is outside of his lovely big white house mowing his lawn. The narrator (in a low voice like that of the Allstate spokesperson) says something like, "This is Ted. Ted has a beautiful four-bedroom house in a desirable suburb, has a pool, has a luxury sedan, and vacations in Hawaii every year. How does he do it?"

Then Ted turns to the camera and says with a smile, "I'm in debt up to my eyeballs."

I think of that commercial often when I sit with a certain type of client: she makes good money as a nurse, she's got a new Lexus SUV, her husband has a newish BMW, he has a fine income as well. Together they make, let's say, one hundred fifty thousand dollars a year. They live in a large four-bedroom house in an established gated community. They have three grown children, whom they put through college. She sometimes works the night shift to make extra money. They vacation at least three times a year in exotic locations. They are carrying credit card debt of about fifteen thousand dollars and have next to nothing saved for retirement.

I watch her work so hard, sacrificing her health in many ways to make more and more money, and yet she has little to show for it. Yes, she has the house, with a $300,000 mortgage still outstanding. She has the cars, but they are unlikely to retain any value after the leases are up, and she will likely end up having to pay more for going over the mileage limit. The two of them are nearing retirement age, so their options to save are becoming more and more limited with each passing day.

What else can you gather about this couple? They have been living beyond their means for years. The best they can do is to begin to simplify their life. They need to drastically cut back on their spending and bring their monthly expenses down below what Social Security and whatever the proceeds from the sale of their house may provide when they get to retirement.

There are many variables at work here, but the point is that in order to know where you will end up, you have to get a handle on your expectations for the life you want to live later on. No one wants to live in poverty when they are older, retired, and perhaps unable to work.

This scenario has become a way of life for many, many people—too many people. It's become the norm to live to work. We spin our wheels working to pay for all the pretty things that ultimately will be our undoing if we can't get ahead of the colossal debt wave.

Look at your budget and what you have been able to uncover. Make some decisions about where you can reduce your spending. Perhaps revisit the cellular store and negotiate a lower-rate plan. Maybe you can live in a smaller apartment, house, or condo just as comfortably as you do now. Maybe you can move to a different area with a lower cost of living. Maybe you can renegotiate your contract or salary at work.

Maybe you can trade some of those higher-interest credit cards for low-rate balance transfer cards—or even a 0 percent card if you have reasonably good credit. (Go to www.bankrate.com to check on offers.) Maybe you can skip the Starbucks coffee four times a week and treat yourself on Fridays. Maybe you resolve to learn to cook at home rather than eat out so often. Maybe you can take a deep breath, smile, take a reasonable, ready-to-compromise look at your expenses, and get serious about reducing your spending.

Whatever you do, wherever you can cut, you will be thankful that you did when you see your savings really start to accumulate! I promise you. Then once you've got your budget all set and you know where your savings is going to come from, you can start to build your financial plan. But you have to cover the basics—and budgeting is the most basic financial exercise and often the most critical. (Yes, I realize it's a chore. That's what the wine is for.)

The Mystery of Credit, or Dr. Jekyll and Mr. Hyde

Now comes the talk you've been waiting for about the love-hate relationship we all have with that wily two-faced financial tool (crutch?) known as credit. You knew this was coming. The truth is, there are some basic and incredibly simple rules to follow that will help you avoid the pitfalls of credit. Once you've mastered following these rules, you may graduate to using credit in your favor. I will go into more detail about how to optimize your credit and make it really work for you by using the benefits of what credit has to offer without falling prey to the many hazards that can trip you up if you're not careful. To be sure, this topic is a critical one to understand if you are to gain true financial independence. So let's start here, now, with the basics.

A Slippery Slope

Credit can be a tricky mistress (or mister) if you aren't careful with it. The temptation to buy something you can't really afford just because the credit is readily available can be overwhelming. You know this scene: You step into an auto showroom. The air is crisp with the scent of jasmine. It's a spa-like atmosphere meant to draw you in and lose yourself. An attractive young person casually walks up and offers you an espresso or a Perrier. Soon you're ushered to a shiny leather seat by the window overlooking a 2019 Audi R8 Spyder glistening in the sun, beckoning you for a test drive. Just one little spin. What could it hurt? You feel heady, also feeling the pull of yearning.

You *could* do it. You work hard. You make a decent salary. You deserve it. The financing is there. It's not altogether reasonable, but it's there. You could make it work. You would look so good in that car. The lovely salesperson, knowing the exact dilemma playing out in your mind, says on cue, "You can lease it for forty-eight months for only eight hundred ninety-nine dollars a month." You know that it's wrong, but it feels so right. Here it is, the moment of truth. What do you do?

Suddenly, a newborn cries and you snap out of it. Your wife, holding your newborn baby boy, is squinting at you with a look that says, *Don't even freakin' think about it!* You turn to the nice salesperson, give them a smile, and politely excuse yourself, declining the offer. Then, on your way out with your family by your side, you reflect on the opportunity to fantasize for a fleeting moment and silently cheer because you got a free Perrier! What were you doing at the Audi dealer in the first place?!

In all seriousness, this scene plays out every day in stores of all kinds, all across the United States, for trinkets, baubles, and luxuries of every shape and size, the opportunities to overspend too innumerable to count. Purchases as small as a pack of gum to those as large as homes, vehicles, and vacations are made with the swipe of a card and with barely a second thought. It seems to have become fundamental to the American way of life to spend money we don't have. Few things make us feel better than exercising the power of getting something we want. The marketing juggernaut, the onslaught of commercial messages, both subliminal and overt, and the institutional appeal aimed at you for the singular purpose of having you part ways with your cash all have this in mind. I say enough of that limited bankrupt thinking. We need to fix our understanding of money so that our financial house is in order no matter what. It's not hard, but it does take intention. And it takes right decision-making.

I have nothing against Audis personally. They are beautiful cars, and maybe someday when I have the means, I might just settle down and buy one (wink, wink). At present I am too fickle to spend that much on something I might no longer care for in a few years. Plus, I'm not that into stuff right now. Have you figured that out about me yet? I spend money on adventures, experiences, and travel. Less stuff, more life. It has become my mantra lately. I figure that while I have the desire, energy, and health to do it, I had better get to it.

The one thing I do not do is spend money I don't have. I won't go out and saddle myself with crushing debt that turns me into essentially an indentured servant to my material wants. I don't want to have to work to pay for a lack of self-control. I don't want to be married to a mortgage. I believe that my quality of life has tremendous value. There is value in work, but I don't want to have to work myself to death just to pay for stuff. I want to enjoy my life and also have nice things and go to cool places. We are brought up to believe in the American dream: the white picket fence, two-point-five kids, a dog, and a German automobile in the driveway. I want to challenge that idea. I think we need to build from the ground up, not start at the top and fill in the holes later on. Makes sense, right?

Now, I know what you're thinking: *But, Tree, how am I supposed to enjoy life if I never spend on the things that I want? I have so little time as it is. How am I supposed to get any enjoyment out of life?* I am here to assure you that delayed gratification is not an absence of gratification. Soon you are going to have more fun than you've had in a very long time. And that is because you'll have money in the bank, your bases will be covered, you'll be sleeping better, and you'll find yourself in a spot eventually where you do have disposable income that's yours to play with. Now, you might choose to put that money away too. Or you might choose to spend it.

You can adjust your lifestyle based on what you want to do with your money. You need to step away from the small and fleeting satisfaction of instant gratification and look at what makes you truly happy in your life. Money can only make you happy (in the truest sense of the word) if you use it wisely toward achieving your goals. If you're twenty-five and your goal is to retire at fifty-five, but you make around sixty thousand dollars and drive a Porsche, your goals and actions are not in alignment.

So, we start here, now, with the first important question you have to ask when considering the use of credit, which is, what are your life goals? Then answer, "How do you want to live? Do you want to breathe easy and backstroke through life, or do you want to feel as if you're constantly treading water?" Then comes, "How important is that new gadget? And to whom?" These are the questions you must ask yourself.

Another important question to ask when considering credit is, what part of your current income is truly available to repay the financed goods or services? If you don't know the answer to this off the top of your head, then you should ultimately decide not to make the purchase. No, you can't buy that thing. No, you can't put it on credit.

Think of it this way: by keeping tighter reins on your cash flow, you are essentially paying yourself for the time and effort you've spent earning the money. You are valuing money as much as or more than what you can exchange it for. In doing so, you will soon see that money itself is more valuable (since, after all, money earns money).

You should take pride in living within your means. You know your finances and you know what you can afford. If you get caught up trying to impress your neighbor with the latest stuff, it will catch up with you. You may impress others outwardly, but what kind of suffering have you inflicted on yourself by struggling under the weight of that debt? Why is the attention of others more important to you than the feeling of ease within yourself? These are also questions you must ask yourself before taking on debt, along with, what's your motivation?

The worst-case scenario is that the happiness is gone and the bill remains. You know this happens. I can think of a few friends who went all out on a mega diamond engagement ring only to get divorced two years later. The bill likely outlasted the relationship. That's just sad. Even worse is that it will never matter how much money you spend or what you buy—there will always be someone with something bigger, newer, and presumably better. *Always*. And the absolute worst part is who wins. Guess who this is? You got it: the *big* banks. They loaned you the money, and they will get it back. You get the pitfall and they get the plunder—and that is when credit turns on you.

So, When Should You Use Credit?

Ultimately you want to end up owing money to no one so that you can be truly free to do what you want. But when things pop up along the way that seem to be needs or must be financed, when considering the use of credit ask yourself, what is the absolute maximum amount that you can reasonably afford to repay should the worst-case scenario fall upon you? How can you quickly and easily calculate this? You estimate your disposable income (you should know it after doing your budget!) and compare it to the payment options, interest rate, and length of the credit term. If the terms are favorable and you can easily afford the payments even if you were to lose your job or become temporarily sick or disabled, or if you could afford to pay off the balance completely within a very short amount of time, you may use credit for the purchase. In fact, there are some big purchases that actually make more sense to finance. I'll go into greater detail about these a little later, but for now, let's talk about good debt and bad debt. Yes, there is such a thing as a good debt.

You should use these sets of questions when considering taking on any debt, especially **good debt**. Knowing the difference between good debt and bad debt is another key thing to know when taking back your credit power. Good debt is an investment; it will return value over time. **Bad debt** is a liability; it only costs you more over time and has little to no value by the time you finish paying it off. Remember our definition of investment: "anywhere you put your money where you expect it to grow."

You can acquire an investment through debt and also through a cash purchase. When you purchase a house (with a mortgage that you can reasonably repay), you expect that house to appreciate in value over time. Therefore, the mortgage you apply for in order to purchase the house would be, in most situations, an example of good debt. There are certain types of mortgages that can be bad debt, but in general, home mortgages are traditionally thought of as good debt. Education or college loans are generally thought of as good debt, assuming that you are acquiring skills through the education you're financing that would enable you to earn a greater income after graduation than you otherwise would. If you finance college and pursue a degree that has no potential for greater earnings after graduation, or if you don't finish college at all but still have the loans, it could be considered bad debt because the return on investment would be nil or negative. In that case, it might be better to spend your time and money on work experience. But generally, people go to school or college in order to become better qualified for jobs with greater income potential.

Following is a general list of examples of good and bad debt, but this list is not absolute. You may have already caught on to the fact that everything in finance is situational.

Good debt	Bad debt
House	Car
Education	Credit cards

| Business | Time-share |
| Real estate | Boat |

Basically, if you finance something that has little to no value after you are finished paying for it, it's considered bad debt. That's a good rule of thumb for discerning which is which.

I will also say that the closer you get to reaching your goals of financial independence and ultimate freedom, the less you should elect to use other people's money and obligate yourself to a long-term repayment plan. That is simply counterintuitive. The closer you are to retirement, if that is one of your goals, the less debt you should carry and the more you ought to be in control of your expenses.

Like I said, it is easy to get caught up in the moment, sign on the dotted line, and go home with a shiny new toy. We've all been there. The problems arise when you do that to the point where you can no longer afford to pay back the money you borrowed and the interest it has accumulated. Credit is not "free money," and you can't outrun it. You can't hide from it. And it can have major backlash if your credit score is negatively affected. Yes, you have a credit score whether you know it or not, and every decision you make with regard to credit can positively or negatively affect it. That's a lot of pressure, so let's try to demystify it a little.

The bottom line is, credit is not evil. It's a necessary part of life. You just need to exercise some self-control and have a good understanding of your budget to be able to use credit to your advantage. Credit can open doors for you that might never open if you only pay cash for everything in your life. Plus, credit is protected from theft and unauthorized use. *Pro Tip:* Download a credit-monitoring app. There are plenty of free ones out there that can get you started on tracking, protecting, and optimizing your credit. Nerd Wallet and Credit Karma are just two examples that come to mind, but you can use whatever you like.

The Illustrious Credit Score

Now let's take a moment to talk about your credit score. Maintaining good credit takes an investment of time. You must look after your credit score and protect it, much like nurturing a plant or a tree. If you keep an eye on it and give it the water and sunlight it needs, then your tree will become strong and you will reap cooling shade and fresh air—the benefits of the tree. Your credit will reflect positively on you and money will flow freely, allowing you greater investment opportunities and better interest rates.

The evolution of credit has had its advantages as well as its disadvantages. Financing something is no longer a taboo practice, but rather a welcome alternative to using your own cash to buy something. It helps keep our economy growing and expanding as well, no doubt. But, as I said before, you should only consider it an alternative if you have thought it through properly with the big picture in mind. With credit, what you must understand is the risk you are taking.

Your creditworthiness is something to be nurtured, protected, and encouraged much like a prized asset, which it certainly is if your credit is good and companies want to lend you money. If you have done a good job keeping yourself out of insurmountable debt, kept up with the payments you owe, and have perhaps paid off a few debts since you became an adult, you will likely have a good **credit score**. Your credit score helps potential lenders evaluate the likelihood that you will repay your debts to them. It also helps you get better deals and creates greater competition among lenders for your business, which helps you get lower interest rates and better terms—both great things for your finances!

You may have heard your credit score referred to as a **FICO score,** which is the most widely used measure of creditworthiness by lenders. It's kind of funny that you are judged as creditworthy based on an arbitrary scale made up by a for-profit company, rather than by the actual cash flow of your income versus your current debts. But that's the way it is. The score is derived from multiple sources that come together to paint a picture of your overall debt-to-income ratio and payment history. The higher your score, the more likely you will be granted higher and higher debt limits. And get this: if you have a lot of available credit but don't use much of it, you are more likely to be approved for more credit! Like I said, it's a funny world we live in.

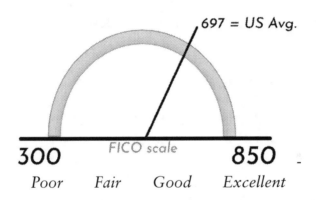

The bottom line here is this: *It is up to you to make sure you do not overdo it with borrowing money.* Only you will truly know whether you can afford to pay back what you borrow. You have to keep your **debt-to-income ratio** in mind. Your debt-to-income ratio is the amount of money you owe versus the amount of money you bring in. If you can consistently keep your monthly total debt payments to one-third of your income, then you are doing pretty well. US banks prefer that housing-to-income payments stay between 28 percent and 33 percent on average. That doesn't tell the whole story, however. A 2015 *Fortune* magazine article[2] noted that:

> "The average U.S. household, by comparison, owed $204,992 in mortgages, credit cards, and student loans in mid-2015 on a median household income of $55,192, according to data compiled by Sentier Research."

That's a 370 percent debt-to-income ratio! The lower your debt-to-income ratio, the more likely you will be able to pay back your debts and the more likely you will have extra money to save and grow your **net worth**. Your net worth, or sometimes called your "nest egg," is your basic measurement of wealth. Simply put, it's like this:

What you own – What you owe = Your net worth

When you are considering taking on debt, whether to buy a house or a car or anything really, you have to be diligent and reasonable in your estimation of likely payback. It's not just up to the lender to deem you creditworthy. You must deem yourself able to pay the money back with reasonable ease. A good way to test for yourself if you are able to take on a debt is to ask yourself, "If I were to lose my job tomorrow, could I still afford to continue to repay this loan?" If the answer is yes, the next question is "For how long?" Never make the decision to borrow money based on the best-case scenario; do it based on the worst possible case. Base it on your what-if scenario. If you can still comfortably afford to continue repaying the loan for some time, then you may be in a good position to use someone else's money to purchase something rather than use your own. Don't just take money some bank is willing to loan you, do your due diligence

---

[2] S.Kumar, "3 Reasons the average American may be worse off than Greece", *Fortune*, July 9, 2015.

and make sure you can reasonably pay back the debt and if it makes sense to finance a purchase now or wait until terms are more favorable for you. Just because the money is there, doesn't mean it's a great idea to take it.

The truth is, it is difficult to live a credit-free life. Credit infiltrates almost every aspect of an American adult's lifestyle. They check your credit to turn on your electricity. They check your credit to rent you an apartment or house. They check your credit to sell you a car. They check your credit to sell you car insurance. It is never-ending. That being said, once you have poor to fair credit, it can be difficult to erase that damage permanently. But you can improve your credit score by going back to the basics. You first need to make arrangements with your creditors and share with them your plan to pay them back. If you absolutely cannot pay them back—and I hate this idea, but it is sometimes necessary in the most desperate of situations— you have the option to file for bankruptcy. Keep in mind, even a bankruptcy cannot erase some debts, especially those held by the government. Some people use this option as a "get-out-of-jail-free card" and repeatedly file for bankruptcy, never changing their behavior. I think this is despicable. If you are a grown adult and if you can purchase something on credit, you can either pay the money back or give the item back, period. I know that no one who would repeatedly file for bankruptcy would bother to read a book like *Money Moves*, so that statement certainly wasn't aimed at you. The average household credit card debt in the United States is more than fifteen thousand dollars! We all know people out there using (and abusing) credit. A bankruptcy stays on a person's credit report for a minimum of seven years. Other loan defaults may stay on there for three years or longer. Government debts are never removed and may result in garnishment of your paycheck or tax refund if you refuse to pay back a government debt or do not come up with an agreeable repayment plan with good old Uncle Sam.

If you find yourself with a less than stellar credit score and you'd like to improve it, you can follow a few simple steps to make a big impact on your credit down the line. Sometimes you have to take a few steps backward to correct your position so that you may move forward freely. I've had to do this, and it can be painful, but you can do it! Here we go:

Ten Steps to Improving Credit

Look at your current outstanding debt. How are you handling repayment? Is it a struggle? Are you late on any payments? Are any of your loans in default? Knowing what we've already talked about, do you see any opportunity for consolidation or transfer to a lower interest rate?

1. Negotiate with your creditors for a lower interest rate, perhaps in exchange for a balance transfer or consolidation of other credit card or loan balances.
2. Cut up any cards you currently don't use but that may have a balance.
3. Call your creditors and lower your credit limits or turn off your cards for further purchases. Don't accept any automatic increases to your credit limit. You can decline them by calling your issuer.
4. Cancel any cards that you don't absolutely need, especially store-issued credit (such as Victoria's Secret or Sharper Image) that typically comes with an interest rate of 20 percent or more regardless of your credit score.
5. Go to www.bankrate.com and look for a 0 percent credit card or a balance transfer offer if you are unable to get any from your current credit card providers.
6. After you have consolidated your debts to as few as possible, look at your minimum required payments on your new balances. When you pay these bills, send in

more than is required. It doesn't matter if it is only ten dollars more, it will help you pay down your debt faster.

7. Don't run up any more debt! Go back to your budget, trim the fat, get rid of anything that is not essential, and cancel nonessential things at least for a little while until you are able to pay off your debt. It makes no sense to be paying for cable TV, a gym membership, or weekly restaurant meals if you have debt up to your eyeballs. Sacrifice a few luxuries for a little while until you can get a grip on your finances, and then revisit the luxuries when you can really afford them. You can free up some money somewhere; everyone can. A little sacrifice now goes a long way later.

8. Stick to your plan to pay off your debt. It may take three to five years. Stick to it! There is no better feeling than being truly free with your money. It will be worth it!

9. If you are saving in your retirement plan, a savings account or somewhere else, consider lowering your savings rate for a brief period so you can pay off your debt in as little time as possible. If your employer matches your retirement contributions, lower your savings rate to the maximum that they match. If you're saving money for a rainy day in some account that is earning less than one percent, it makes no sense to keep that up while you're paying a credit card company 16% on your balance there. Pay it off and then go back to saving, you could probably afford to put a little more away towards whatever your savings goals are now that you don't have that debt and interest weighing you down!

10. Celebrate every little triumph! When you have paid off one card but you have three to go, give yourself a pat on the back and keep up the good work! It only gets better. Once you are no longer carrying a balance on your credit cards and your long-term loans are steadily being paid down with more than the minimum, you

can begin to reap the benefits of using credit to your advantage. Your credit score will automatically improve with regular overpayment and the eventual payoff of most of your available credit. It happens automatically when you practice good habits.

What I suggest here is not an exhaustive cure-all for credit. There will be plenty of people or agencies out there trying to get you to hire them to "fix your credit." Some are legitimate; some are not. And they all cost money—money that could be going toward paying down your debt yourself, instead of risking it with some company that may or may not be able to help. The bottom line is this: *You have to change your behavior if you are truly going to fix your credit woes.* You don't want to fix your credit this year and then end up in the same position five years down the road just because you didn't address the issue underlying your spending habits. If you don't have the money to buy something, just don't buy it. The banks, however, are betting against you, and the stats support their bet. Let's prove them wrong, shall we?

Using Credit to Your Advantage

Now that your credit is in good health (or at least you are well on your way to healthy credit!) and you have a firm grasp on when you may be able to take on new debt, you have the option of considering credit for its advantages. You've surely heard people say, "You need money to make money" or "The best way to make money is to use someone else's." These sayings are true, but these practices don't always work out the way we'd like them to. You have to be extra careful when you use someone else's money to try to build wealth for yourself. In fact, your ability to access money and grow wealth may be affected for years to come. I'm not going to sit here and tell you not to use credit. I am a practical, realistic person who knows that sometimes the best way to get ahead is to borrow some money now and pay it back later. But if you're going to take this route, you must be clear on the consequences.

If you don't properly care for your credit, if you neglect doing your due diligence, and if you abuse credit by running up your balances and not paying them down, then your credit will begin to behave badly. It will reflect poorly on you and will limit your access not only to investments, but also to everyday essentials such as housing, bank accounts, utilities, and insurance. Access to these things is critical for properly protecting your assets, your hard-earned money, and your loved ones. Yes, your credit can affect your ability to properly care for and provide for your loved ones. It is a risk-and-reward scenario that you must be crystal clear about.

Your credit is very important. Of course, it's great to pay for everything with cash, but you can use credit to your advantage and even gain wealth from its proper use. When you use someone else's money to purchase something, it frees up your own money for other things in the short term and allows you to pay back the borrowed money over an extended period. The time you have to pay it back, any restrictions or rules, and the fee to use someone else's money (the interest you pay) comprise what is referred to as the **terms** of the loan. If you don't like the terms of the loan, you can shop other potential lenders for better terms. But be careful! The more lenders that check your credit, the more cautious the next ones become about lending money to you. Yes, they can see who else is checking your credit. They start to question what may be happening if you have too many recent inquiries on your credit report. And yes, these hard inquiries affect your score.

Sometimes, depending on the marketplace and the overall economy, lenders will be very eager and willing to loan out money. Other times, depending on their particular financial situation, they may not be so willing, and therefore you may hear people say things like "Money is tight" or "Banks aren't lending right now." The latter may or may not be true depending on the bank, the regulations, and the prevailing interest rates in the marketplace. Some companies may be seeking to loan more money, whereas other companies may have a different strategy.

For instance, back in 2004–6, money was very easy to come by. Banks were lending huge amounts of money to people for home purchases and the like. Many of my clients who were making less than $50,000 per year bought second homes while they still had a mortgage on the first. I thought it was quite odd and unsustainably risky. At the time, there had been a significant easing on bank regulations and an increase in the amount of money that banks were able to lend. In addition, many mortgages were being underwritten in creative ways other than the typical thirty-year fixed mortgage (same rate for the whole term) or fifteen-year ARM (adjustable rate mortgage, where the rate can change over time). We saw "stated income mortgages" that were being written not through proof of income, but by people simply making a statement about their potential income and the banks basically taking them at their word. It was unusual, to say the least. It was a time of seemingly free money. Anyone could get a loan for a huge amount and little down payment, little proof of income required, and no safety net. I know you saw those 103 percent financing terms. That means people were either getting money back for buying a house or were including their closing costs with the actual purchase price of the house—and *no money down*. Those buyers had no skin in the game other than the risk of foreclosure and the destruction of their credit. It's no wonder people took what they could get!

In my world, if I cannot continue to repay my obligations even if the worst should happen, I do not take on additional debt. If you plan for the worst and hope for the best, you'll usually end up somewhere in the middle, but you will be protected if the worst does hit. It comes back to that #1 cardinal rule of money: *live within your means!*

Was it alluring for some people who were able to buy homes

at preconstruction prices and then turn around and sell them (or "flip" them) for a profit a few months later? Of course! But it was also very risky. The problems arose when the housing market slowed and those people were stuck with a house, a new mortgage, and rapidly falling home prices. That is the worst-possible-case scenario, and it happened! So, naturally, we had an influx of foreclosures and short sales, and a declining housing market, for many years. I still don't believe the housing has totally recovered in many areas of the country. If you were one of the unfortunate buyers who got in when the market was at its peak, you very likely had to declare bankruptcy to get out from under your debt.

On the flip side, the housing bubble crash created an opportunity for those who had cash and were sitting on the sidelines and who saw that what was happening was unsustainable. Those people were able to go in and buy up foreclosed properties at a fraction of the price of what they had sold for merely a year or two earlier.

As you can see from the foregoing example, credit can either make you or break you. If your credit is good to great, then more opportunities for investment open up. If your credit is fair to poor, then you need to first work on repairing it before you try to make any large investment decisions. Somewhere along the line you will have to get someone to help you finance your investments, which will be a whole lot easier if you have good credit. So, let's talk a little bit more about using credit the right way.

There are several types of credit out there, and nearly all of them affect your credit score. Among credit terms, you'll find long-term credit, short-term credit, revolving credit, fixed rate credit, and variable rate credit. All of them are important, so we'll go into some detail about each so that you know the difference and where and when you should use each type.

Long-Term Credit

Long-term credit is usually any loan term that is set for repayment over a period of five years or more. As we've been discussing, a mortgage is obviously a long-term credit instrument. It's a large loan collateralized by a piece of property—a house for most people. Mortgages can come in many different year terms but most commonly are issued for repayment over a ten-year, fifteen-year, or thirty-year term. Mortgages can have a fixed or variable interest rate for the repayment term. If you default on a mortgage or don't pay it back, it is referred to as a foreclosure. Other long-term loans can be arranged to pay for higher education, commercial property, land purchases, large equipment purchases, and some luxury items. Long-term credit loans typically have a set payment schedule and rules and restrictions for prepayment, reamortization (adjusting the repayment schedule), and refinancing (adjusting the terms of the loan). Vehicles, machinery, and business equipment may also be financed for purchase through long-term credit arrangements.

Short-Term Credit

Short-term credit is usually any loan term that is set for repayment in five years or less. Think of your typical car loan or sometimes a home equity loan, a personal loan, or any type of store credit financing. These loans have a short payback period. And because of the shorter time frame to make money, interest rates for preferred credit applicants must stay close to prevailing market rates for prime customers. Many times you will find promotional rate periods with furniture stores, car dealerships, and appliance retailers who want to lure you in with the promise of 0 percent down or perhaps 0 percent financing for a set number of months. These deals can be a great tool if you pay the debt within the prescribed period. If you fail to do so, the interest rate upon default or at the expiration of the promotional period usually skyrockets to well beyond prevailing market interest rates. Be very mindful of your payment schedule if you take advantage of one of these deals. You will lose all the benefit of the deal the second you fail to keep up your end of the agreement.

Revolving Credit

Revolving credit is essentially a credit card or a credit line that you pay off and reuse over and over again. It is ideal to use a credit card and pay it off every month unless you are using a promotional offer for 0 percent interest over a specified period. The best credit cards for helping you take advantage of your great credit habits are rewards cards. With these, you get paid for using your credit card for your everyday purchases—stuff you would buy anyway. The trick is to set aside that money you would have spent to be sure you'll have enough at the end of the month to pay the credit card balance in full. This way, you don't increase your spending, you pay no interest, and you receive some handsome rewards. If you can keep ahead of your balance for a year, and depending on how much you spend every month, you could end up paying for a vacation, an experience, or even a whole month's credit card payment with your accumulated rewards.

However, you *must* stay on top of your credit cards to make sure you're not falling prey to using them because it is easy to do so. Don't get sucked into the cycle of running up a balance and carrying it over every month. You'll trigger the interest rate that way, which will essentially make your rewards worthless. The credit card companies are hoping you'll slip up. That's why they offer the rewards in the first place. But good cardholders know they can get something for nothing if they play their cards right! Just be careful if you're going to try this out. It's easier if you have very few credit cards. That's why I advocate keeping your favorite cards with the best rewards and getting rid of the rest. Don't even tempt yourself.

A HELOC, or home equity line of credit, is also a form of revolving credit as long as the bank continues to leave it open and accessible to you. Keep in mind, the bank can reduce the amount of, restrict, and/or close your HELOC at any time without your consent. When this happens, it has a negative effect on your overall credit score and can negatively impact your ability to gain credit in the near future. Remember when I said that the more credit you have available (and unused), the more likely you are to be approved for more credit? This procedure speaks directly to that. Banks may want to limit their exposure to debt risk if there are declining market values on real estate, so they will periodically review their open HELOCs and their home equity loan balances and adjust the available credit according to the amount of risk they need to reduce. I know this sounds weird, but it has happened to me—and it comes as a shock when you first realize what is happening, if you catch it at all. My lender really didn't alert me or make any fanfare about it; they just reduced the amount of credit available to me, which in turn reduced my credit score because it looked as if I was using up more of my available credit than I had done previously. Yes, in fact, I was using more as a percentage overall, but I had not increased my outstanding debt. As you can probably tell, I was not very pleased about it, but so it goes. Live and learn, and pay it forward!

Let me illustrate this point a little more clearly with an example:

Jane has a home worth $250,000. Her current outstanding mortgage is $110,000. Her bank sends her a promotional flyer offering a home equity line of credit (HELOC) for her to use as she wishes for up to $100,000 at a 3 percent APR (annual percentage rate) of interest. Jane was thinking about remodeling her kitchen and decided to take out $20,000. After ten months of timely payments and a new kitchen, Jane receives a letter in the mail saying that the bank is reducing her available HELOC to $40,000. Jane is suddenly curious about what that means for her otherwise stellar credit score. What do you think?

Because Jane took out the $20,000 when her available HELOC was $100,000, she was only using 20 percent of her available credit. This is generally a good percentage for your score; you want to keep it below 33 percent as a rule of thumb. Despite Jane's on-time payments and commitment to only taking out the $20,000, her credit usage rate went up to close to 50 percent when her bank reduced her available credit to $40,000, dinging her credit score. It was not Jane's fault that her credit score went down. You must keep in mind that many factors beyond your control can improve or damage your credit score. You must also be aware of the effect that seemingly harmless inquiries, adjustments, and scenarios could potentially have on your score and try to foresee these situations. You can't prevent everything from affecting your credit, but you can be aware of the potential pitfalls if you decide to apply for credit in any form.

Fixed Rate Credit

This is a term used for credit that you obtain that has a specified fixed interest rate. A loan or credit card can have a fixed interest rate or one that fluctuates based on certain conditions of the credit agreement. A fixed-interest mortgage will have a specified rate at the time of purchase, and the rate will stay the same throughout the term of your loan. Usually, credit cards have a fixed interest rate on purchases, balance transfers, and cash advances, but they may not all be the same rate, even with the same card, so look over your card agreement very carefully. The rates are typically different for certain transactions. If you use the cash advance or cash access feature of your credit card, it will typically cost you a much higher rate of interest—close to a loan shark rate. So, here's a tip: Never use this. I repeat: never use the cash advance feature on your credit card. There are other ways to access cash that won't cost you an arm and a leg. It is much more preferable to use the balance transfer check that the credit card company will inevitably send to you if you do not use the credit they have extended to you to their liking. They do that to persuade you to use the available credit. Usually, it is a very good interest rate for a set amount of time. This feature makes sense to use if you are paying other loans or debts with higher interest rates and you can be sure you will pay off the balance within the promotional rate period. Be very careful here too, because if you fail to pay the card on time or if you are late on a payment, the card issuer may increase the interest rate dramatically and without any extra warning outside of the credit agreement that they are required to send every year.

Variable Rate Credit

Variable rate credit is just as it sounds. It is a rate that depends on factors in the credit term agreement, usually based on the prevailing market rates for a period of time and perhaps involving a rate hike after a certain number of years or a balloon payment at some point. You may find variable rate credit in short-term loans, long-term loans, credit cards, HELOCs, and other such loans. The rate fluctuates, which in some market situations can be more attractive than a fixed rate credit agreement. For example, back in the 1980s when interest rates were extremely high, it was more attractive to get an adjustable rate mortgage (ARM) for a home purchase than to be locked into a fifteen- or thirty-year fixed rate mortgage at 15 percent interest for the life of the loan, or having to face refinancing sometime in the near future. Banks were paying interest around 13 percent on savings accounts. For a first-time home buyer, a $100,000 home would cost $15,000 for the first year of interest payments alone with no principal repayment. At that same time, you could get an ARM for around 8 percent for the first five years with a readjustment in year five to the market rate at that time. The risk for the home buyer in this scenario is that the prevailing interest rate could have risen higher and he or she would then be locked in after five years to an even higher monthly mortgage payment. However, for that same first-time home buyer, interest payments came down to $8,000 per year, so much more of his or her monthly mortgage payment could go toward paying down the principal of the loan. Luckily for first-time home buyers, the interest rate environment eased up during the recession in the late 1980s to the early 1990s and the rate lock ended up in their favor many times, but of course, hindsight is 20/20.

Whether you utilize fixed or variable rate credit, you must always pay attention to the prevailing market rates, the ease of gaining access to more debt based on your credit score, the availability of money, the willingness of banks to loan out money, and your ability to pay back what you borrow. Run the numbers. If it's too complicated for you to understand, do not accept the terms. What I'm saying is, if a bank offers you a loan but you can't clearly understand the terms of the loan, then do not take the loan. Read the fine print, and never sign anything you don't understand. When it comes to a large purchase such as a home, employ a good lawyer to translate the paperwork and negotiate the terms with your best interests in mind. The small extra investment is well worth it. When you go to buy a home and you know that you can reasonably afford a $1,500-per-month mortgage payment with a 5 percent down payment (even if you lost your job for a period of time), don't let someone talk you into buying a home for $2,000 a month and 10 percent down. Tell your realtor your budget, and make sure he or she sticks to it.

If you can't make the numbers work in the worst-possible-case scenario, do not take on the additional debt. Also remember to revisit and check on your debt, your interest rates, and your credit score periodically. It is vitally important that you stay on top of the big picture with your credit. Interest rates change, and credit agreements can change without your input. And with the prevalence of identity theft these days, your credit score can change. Check on all these factors at least annually. It's an easy thing to do these days with convenient apps such as Nerd Wallet and Credit Karma to help you.

I recommend checking over the rewards, benefits, and interest rates of your credit cards annually as interest rates and rewards programs can change rapidly. Credit card issuers will often negotiate with long-standing well-paying cardholders. If you find a better deal somewhere else, then before you switch credit cards, close any accounts, or open new ones, you should talk to your current card providers and see what they can do for you. If they can't (or won't) do anything for you, then feel free to take your business elsewhere. Yes, closing a credit account does have an effect on your credit score, but the impact is much smaller than if you fail to pay on time, were denied for credit, or defaulted on a loan. The life of your credit history is only one factor that helps determine your overall credit score, but in my opinion, it is more important to use your credit wisely, know your limits, and keep your credit safe from predators.

Along these lines, I research the best-reviewed rewards cards and align them with what I would appreciate and realistically use in my life. Not everyone travels on Southwest Airlines, so a Southwest Airlines rewards card may not be ideal for you. But if you do travel on Southwest, that card may be the most attractive one to you. Alternatively, you may want a cash-back card because you'd like more freedom when using rewards. That is your prerogative. You need to find the best rewards card for you and use it in a way to gain the greatest possible benefit without getting into credit trouble.

Keeping the number of credit cards that you own and actually use to below three is ideal. I know there are different lifestyles and situations out there, so many people will need a gas card, a rewards card, and perhaps a store card. Keep in mind, the more cards you have available to you, especially on your person at any given time, the more likely you are to buy on impulse. Keep the number of cards you own and have available to a minimum. I carry and use only one credit card and my debit card. Pick your few favorites and cut up the rest. Simplify your life, and you will see the benefits flood at you tenfold or more. I promise you.

I will note here that I am guilty of applying for credit just to get a good deal on a large purchase and simply paying off the credit card and then closing the account immediately afterward. Think Target, think Kohl's, think Brooks Brothers. What can I say? If I do *have* to shop, at the very least I am going to get a good deal!

Creating a Financial Road Map— the Solid Foundation for a Clear Future

Now that the boring budgeting business is over with (good riddance!) and we've discussed how to get your credit to work for you instead of against you, it's time to create a solid but simple financial plan. You want your financial plan to be easy to understand and easy to execute. You also need it to be flexible. Simplicity fulfills all these requirements. Some expenses will inevitably pop up out of nowhere; your plan needs to allow for those unexpected turns. Life happens. It just does. It throws you curveballs and sliders and presents all kinds of weird changeups, but in the end, if you have a flexible, simple financial plan, you'll be ready for whatever might happen.

A Solid Foundation for a Clear Future

I know it might sound hokey, but this is a very important moment in your path toward financial health. It is the equivalent of planning your meals for the week when you're aiming for better nutrition, or setting a schedule of weekly exercise when striving for physical fitness. A financial plan has some standard components, but it is also unique to you. The work we've done to identify your why and the areas of life that are most important to you is now going to guide your approach to this next step.

The first step toward financial freedom is to create a solid foundation. You do this by building an emergency fund. Setting aside an emergency fund is as essential as putting down a concrete layer before building a house, later adding walls and a roof. If you have no foundation, you can't effectively build other elements necessary for the house. Without a sturdy foundation, the structure you build is at risk of all kinds of damage and could come crashing down in a moment, even in the tiniest of storms.

An **emergency fund** is a savings account where you keep three to nine months' worth of average monthly expenses (from your budget) ready at a moment's notice. In other words, it's cash. Having money readily available means that it is **liquid. Liquidity** is the ability to turn an asset, security, or other investment into cash quickly. Assets are things you own that have value; investments are assets that you expect to grow in value over time; and a security is a specific type of investment, like a stock or a bond. An asset or investment is said to be liquid if you can cash it in readily, at any time, without restriction or penalty. Conversely, an asset is said to be illiquid if it is difficult or takes considerable time to turn it into cash (usually through a sale).

Think for a moment about the assets you own. What are the restrictions or hurdles you would face if you needed to get the money out of those assets at any time? Which of them are liquid? Which are illiquid?

It is not better or worse to have more liquid than illiquid assets at any given time. The liquidity of your assets only matters if you have obligations that are not covered. If you have an adequate emergency fund to cover your short-term obligations and any sudden unexpected expenses that pop up out of nowhere, then you can have other investments that need to be held for the long term. It is fine if long-term assets are illiquid. In other words, you need a certain amount of cash to cover your expenses and your what-ifs. Following is a list of examples of liquid and illiquid assets:

Liquid assets	Illiquid assets
Cash	House
Savings account	Car
Checking account	Stocks
Money market account	Bonds
Safe deposit box deposits	Retirement savings
Short-term treasury notes	Land
Certificates of deposit (CDs)*	Businesses
	Real Estate
	Art/collectibles
	Jewelry / precious metals

These are just a few examples to give you an idea. Stocks, bonds, and retirement assets may seem liquid, but the liquidity of those funds will depend on a few factors. First, you want to cash in securities such as stocks and bonds when the market for those securities is up, so then you can sell them for more than what you paid for them. If the market is down, or if they are worth less than what you paid, you will have to wait until the market comes back up before you sell or cash out if you wish to realize a profit. If you're stuck and need cash even in a down market, you may be forced to take a loss if you cash out your securities. This means that inherently, they're illiquid.

Your retirement savings is not liquid because of age restrictions and penalties that the IRS imposes for withdrawals from those accounts. If you have to pay a penalty to get your money out prior to reaching age sixty, then you do not have what is considered a liquid asset. That is why I put an asterisk next to certificates of deposit in the earlier list. Some CDs come with restrictions and charge penalties if you fail to leave the money with the bank for a specified amount of time. Other CDs allow withdrawals with no penalties, so it depends on the product and the issuer (banks, in the case of CDs). What you need to consider with your liquid investments is if you can access your money without paying some sort of cost, whether opportunity cost or hard dollars.

It is vitally important to have your emergency fund readily available. As I said before, your emergency fund should have at least three months', but not more than nine months', of your average monthly expenses safely deposited in a liquid account that is easily accessible should a problem arise. No more than nine months' worth of expenses is needed; it is unlikely that you will actually need that much cash on hand at once. If you lose your job, you can typically apply for unemployment. The average time it takes to get another job, according to data from the Bureau of Labor Statistics in September 2019, is twenty-two weeks, or about five months. Of course, this figure has to be adjusted to account for the economy and other factors.

You don't want to park too much of your hard-earned money in something that won't yield much return for an extended period of time, so you need to limit the amount of money you put into your emergency fund. The hard truth is, most people either don't have an emergency fund at all or have one that is vastly inadequate, or what the industry refers to as "underfunded." Many people rely on credit cards, personal or 401(k) loans, and loans from family members to help them out when life's unexpected challenges occur. That is not at all fiscally responsible. If you are constantly hitting your mother up to bail you out of financial trouble, you'll no longer be her favorite!

The truth is that, as in all money matters, building an emergency fund is easy to do by exercising a little discipline over time. Get in the habit of putting a small percentage of your income away in a savings account each time you have new money in your account or each payday. Start to change your thoughts and feelings so that seeing your numbers add up gives you more pride than seeing extra stuff around the house. With a little practice and intention, you will see how fast things change for you. Then next time you get a flat tire, or the baby needs a new car seat, or the dog has to be rushed to the vet, it's no sweat. The most important thing is to get started—and don't stop!

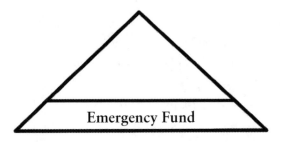

What do you have so far? A solid base. Now you have to think about all the goals, obligations, and future dreams that you want to meet or achieve with your money. Your emergency fund is going to allow your longer-term, illiquid investments to incubate in their respective markets without your having to access them prematurely. If you are forced to access longer-term investments because of an emergency or unexpected expense, you risk either having to sell assets in unfavorable market conditions (selling low) or having to access the equity in your home or real estate before you can finalize a sale. Being forced to liquidate assets before you want to takes away your option to use investments to achieve your goals. When you liquidate as planned, you have greater control over the option to sell and therefore are able to optimize your investment return (profit).

Save, Save, and Save Some More!

The next step in your financial plan is retirement savings. Many people don't realize that retirement will be the single biggest "purchase" they'll ever make in their lives. Think about it—with retirement, you are "buying" thirty years of not working. What would that cost in today's dollars? I'll give you an example:

If you are earning $50,000 per year and you want to quit working for thirty years, it will cost you $1,500,000 to stay out of work for that amount of time ($50,000 × 30 = $1,500,000).

Yes, this is a simplistic example and doesn't account for interest, nor does it consider inflation, but I think you get the point. Retirement ain't gonna be cheap. The best way that you can be sure you'll be able to afford to retire will be to start saving, preferably now. The earlier you start, the better. In fact— and I know I mentioned this in the introduction, but it's worth saying again—ideally you should be saving for your retirement as soon as you get your first job and have earned income. I don't imagine there are too many sixteen-year-olds reading this (if so, good for you! You're way ahead of the curve!), but it remains true that the earlier you get started, the easier it will be for you to reach those lofty goals.

I'll give you another example that might allow you to see how good habits can cause money to add up over time and can tear down what seem like impossible figures pretty quickly.

If you are twenty-five years old earning $30,000 a year and you put 10 percent of your salary in a retirement savings plan earning an average of 8 percent per year, by the time you hit sixty-five, you'll have $777,170. That is a great number. This is also assuming that you never get a raise, you never change your contribution, and you never stop saving. This figure is an adequate amount to retire on, in coordination with Social Security, for someone who is earning $30,000 a year. If you wait until your full Social Security age of sixty-seven to start making retirement plan withdrawals, then you'll have $912,731. That's over one hundred thousand dollars more in just two years, and it's more than thirty years' worth of your salary without any interest (30 years × $30,000 = $900,000)!

You're probably thinking, *I'll save for retirement after I buy a house.* That does seem to be the way most people do it.

Honestly, the way most people do it is totally backward. People go straight from getting their first real job to buying a nicer car, then a nice house. And then they give a fleeting thought to saving for a rainy day or emergency, and somewhere down the line when they realize they're getting older, they take a good look in the mirror and say, "Shit! I haven't saved *anything* for retirement!" Many people have plenty of income, but along with increases in income typically come increases in lifestyle—and that means increases in the bills to support that lifestyle. When you get used to the higher price of a fancier life, you tend to forget about the things you need to plan for and save for down the road. I just don't think that the old conventional way of doing things is going to work for a sound, successful long-term financial plan. Just sayin'!

Saving for retirement is both a lot easier and a lot harder than it used to be. Let me clarify: It's easier because there are ready-made retirement plans offered to you through an investment provider or through your employer that are commonly available everywhere. It's harder because you have to decipher the retirement plan lingo in order to decide which plan, or coordination of plans, is right for you and your goals.

There are a number of vehicles you can use that are tax-favorable, and most large employers offer company retirement plans with contributions that can be deducted directly from your paycheck before you pay income tax. That makes it really easy to save for retirement. You can even set up IRAs (individual retirement accounts) and other vehicles that can draft directly from your bank account if your employer does not offer a plan. A hard part is deciding on one from among a variety of available investment options and vehicles. It can seem overwhelming. Oftentimes I see clients driven to inaction simply because they're afraid to make a mistake or they feel totally clueless about retirement plans or investments in general. *The biggest mistake is not saving at all.* It is always better to save than to save nothing at all. Moreover, if your employer does offer a plan, many times they will contribute for you or match what you put in to some degree. This is what I call "free money" (almost everyone in the industry calls it that), and believe it or not, there are people who do not take it. I know, crazy, right?

I am going to take an in-depth look at the most common retirement plans in chapter 9, but for now let's talk about where we are in our financial road map.

Looking at this pyramid, you can probably guess what comes next. If you guessed a house, you're right! You get a cookie! (No, really, go get a cookie.)

For many people, a house is conventionally thought of as the biggest purchase they'll ever make, especially for those who don't even think about retirement until their midforties or fifties. Considering our prior discussion about retirement, we may have disproven the myth of your house being your largest investment. Yes, I agree that it is still a large purchase. It is also a significant investment. It is significant not only in hard dollars and cents but also to your future ability to access credit, build wealth, and have bargaining leverage for other financial tools should you so choose to use them. When a mortgage company finds you worthy of a loan big enough to buy a house, other possible loan providers take notice. In order to qualify for a mortgage, you must be a reasonably safe bet for the long, long, long term. The most popular mortgage term is thirty years. That's a *long* time. Mortgage companies perform much due diligence to ensure that you can and will fulfill your obligation to them. That's why you have to sign eight to ten inches' worth of paperwork when you finance and purchase a house. You're truly signing away your life, the lives of your children, and the lives of their children in those few moments. Ah, the American dream.

All kidding aside, buying your first home is a significant step toward building wealth and opening doors that might otherwise have taken much longer to open had you waited to establish a long credit history in other ways. Because of the due diligence performed by mortgage lenders (save 2006–8, when anyone could get a mortgage and buy a house with a "stated income." I mean, WTH?), other companies can assume you are more likely to repay your debts and, thus, offer you more credit. I know, it doesn't make much sense, but that is how it works. Like I said, the more available credit you have, the more that lenders offer you. You would expect that based on your income, you would hit a cap and no one would offer you credit above and beyond that. Nope. That's not how it works. Might be why so many US households are pinned beneath grotesque amounts of debt. Just a guess.

Anywho, moving on. Once you've been able to establish yourself as a keen saver with your emergency fund and your retirement savings, and once you have either purchased outright or financed yourself a house, you need to figure out what that tip of the pyramid should be. Truth is, I mostly come across clients who have dabbled a bit in every level but never really fully committed to any one of them. And they're all important. Even with the house purchase, many people don't stick to one house. They jump around, move a lot, and trade up. That makes it very difficult to build equity in such a large maintenance asset.

I call a house a maintenance asset because one constantly has to invest more into its upkeep and preservation to keep it earning money. Houses in and of themselves don't make too much money if they are run down and unkempt or, worse, uninhabited. You need to keep track of all that constant investment to realize your true gain once you sell your house. Many people don't count this, but they should because the ongoing costs of ownership of a house greatly reduce their overall rate of return. I'll go into greater depth when talking about real estate investments in chapter 7.

So, for review: First you set up and fund your emergency account with enough money to cover three to nine months' worth of expenses. Next, you fund your retirement savings to the best of your ability, preferably with 10–15 percent of your salary if you are under age forty-four and 15–20 percent of your salary if you are over age forty-four. If you are starting very late (after fifty), you may need to "power save" even more. I hope your kids are out of the house and out from under your support so that you can do that adequately and without distraction.

If you are having trouble believing that you can save any money, let alone three months' worth for an emergency fund and even more for your retirement plan, let me help you envision being able to save. We already went through your budget, right? You definitely uncovered some places where you can squeeze out a few dollars here and there. Where should you put that money? It depends. Let's work out a few scenarios:

Scenario #1—You're already saving for retirement at a rate above your employer's match. Great! But you have no emergency savings. Go ahead and decrease your contribution temporarily to the maximum match and divert the extra savings to your emergency fund until you have between three and nine months' worth of expenses saved. This may take a year or two, but as long as you are getting the full match from your company, you are doing the right thing. Once your emergency fund is at the right level, go ahead and adjust your retirement contribution back up to your previous contribution level. Just to illustrate this point, let's say you're contributing ten percent of your salary to your 401(k) plan, and your employer matches your contributions to a maximum of six percent. Lower your contribution temporarily to six percent and divert the extra four percent to your emergency fund until you have saved enough to cover six to nine months of your monthly expenses. Then once you have your emergency fund properly funded, return your 401(k) contribution back to ten percent.

Scenario #2—You're saving in your retirement plan and building your emergency fund, but you're paying the minimum monthly payment on your high-interest-rate credit cards. Adjust your retirement plan contribution to the maximum match, reduce your emergency fund savings deposit, and divert more money toward your credit card balances to pay them down quickly. Also, remember when we talked about credit cards in the previous chapter? You may want to consider transferring balances to a promotional-rate card and pay the balance off even faster. Balance transfer tricks can sometimes make you feel that you're playing a shell game, constantly switching from one 0 percent card to the next, but I will tell you that it's a worthy endeavor. Why pay interest if you don't have to? That money could go toward your balance and get it paid off much faster! Trust me, it works!

Scenario #3—You're saving for a house, but you're not saving for retirement or creating an emergency fund. Make sure you are splitting your savings between the three goals in order to maximize long-term results. Meet the match in your retirement plan, save toward three months of expenses in your emergency fund, and keep the rest for the house fund. A house is an expensive asset as I have said time and time again. If you rush to buy a house and you're not yet on solid financial footing, you're setting yourself up for failure. A new roof, a water heater leak, or even Mother Nature can cause your housing costs to skyrocket at any time. Having that emergency fund at the ready will enable you to take care of any problems without unneeded stress. Don't rush it! Set yourself up for success by dividing your savings and not missing out on vital time and help (from your company match) in the process. Time is your best friend when it comes to growing your wealth. The more time you have, the wealthier you'll be if you stick with it!

When I think about saving for retirement, I like to say, "It's time to pay a tithe to the Church of You." You may be the only member of this church, so you've gotta get saving quickly. If you cannot afford to save in every level of your financial plan pyramid just yet, strive to save the most that your company will match at the absolute least. Remember what I said: you don't want to be one of those people who lets his or her employer get away without paying him or her all the free money! If you save less than the maximum amount that the company will match, you are doing just that. And no one else gets that money. It's just a gift that you're giving your company by not taking it.

Let's delve into an example so that it's more visual for you. I want this to be crystal clear.

Mary works for the Banana Company full time. Banana Company offers a 401(k) retirement savings plan to all its full-time employees. Mary wants to participate in the company's 401(k) plan. The company offers a match of 1:1 for each employee, up to 5 percent of the employee's salary. That means that for every dollar Mary puts into her 401(k), Banana will also put in one dollar (a 1:1 match is also called dollar for dollar), up to a maximum of 5 percent of Mary's salary.

If Mary makes $50,000 a year, then 5 percent of her salary is $2,500 ($50,000 × 5% = $2,500). Therefore, if she puts in $2,500 a year, Banana will also put in $2,500 for the year. That is the maximum amount that the company will put in, as long as Mary is compensated $50,000 for the year.

Q. If Mary were to decide to put in $3,000 a year, how much would Banana Company put in?

The answer is $2,500, because the maximum match is up to 5 percent of Mary's salary, which is $2,500.

Q. If Mary were to decide to put in $1,500 per year, how much would Banana Company put in?

The answer is $1,500, because Banana will only match Mary's contribution up to the amount that she puts in, not to the maximum amount, if she doesn't save more. So, $1,500 is only 3 percent of Mary's salary, not the full 5 percent.

Q. So, if Mary puts in $1,500 a year, how much of Banana Company's money is she leaving on the table?

The answer is $1,000 a year, until she increases her contribution to 5 percent of her salary. If she is not contributing at least 5 percent, she is essentially saying, *That's okay, Banana Company, keep your money. I know no one else will get it, but I really don't want your extra thousand dollars a year.*

No one would knowingly say that. *No one* would say no to free money. You have to find a way to save in your retirement savings plan if for no other reason than to get the money the company is willing to give you. If you are having a hard time finding the money to save, go back to the drawing board and reanalyze your budget. Your cell phone company is not giving you free money; neither is your cable company! And don't forget, the money you put in your 401(k) is deducted before you pay income tax, effectively making your tax payment lower. So, you save money, get more money from your company, and pay fewer taxes. The net effect is easier to achieve than you think. It's a win-win-win. There is also an IRS Saver's Credit that the government provides for people who make less than $34,000 for single filers and $68,000 for those married and filing jointly (in 2022). This encourages you to save even more!

This is not just free money; it is instant return without even investing in the market. Read that again.

A 1:1 match is a 100 percent return on your savings. A 2:1 or fifty-cents-per-one-dollar match is 50 percent return on your savings. You can't get that kind of guaranteed return in any type of investment vehicle. Period.

In chapter 9, I will take a deep dive into all the ins and outs of retirement saving options, but right now I want to repeat this very important point so that there is no doubt about what your bare minimum action should be. I know it seems obvious, but I need to drive this message home. You wouldn't believe how many people leave money on the table. I think it's just because they don't really know or they haven't done the math. Well, now you know. And you'll be better for it. PS: *Spread the word!*

That brings me to our last little piece of this pie, the pinnacle, the apex. Once you have adequately and sufficiently funded your emergency fund and your retirement and are paying your mortgage without any problem, you may find yourself in the envious position of having extra money you can save. This would truly be something to celebrate!

Protect What You've Built!

But don't start celebrating yet! (Okay, celebrate a little bit.)

Before you go investing that extra money in a hot stock because of a tip you got from a friend or in your buddy's start-up "adult ice cream" truck company, you need to think about protection. I'm talking about financial protection.

You're well on your way to a sound financial future, and you are sticking to your plan perfectly, but what happens if the plan gets derailed by some unforeseen event? What if the markets tank when you're near retirement? Or what if you lose your job and cannot find another for a *long* time? What happens if you become disabled or, worse, you die? How do you insulate your plan from all the unknowns, what the industry refers to as "contingencies"?

You buy insurance. But how do you know what type of insurance, how much you'll need, and where to get it from? How many types of insurance are there? Do you need all of them? Are all insurance companies created equal? Is insurance mandatory? Let's break this down.

Insurance, like other financial products, is only useful to you when you understand it and know how to use it. First, you've gotta remember that we all make decisions based on what we learn. You do the best you can with the information you have. When you plan for the worst and hope for the best, you come out somewhere in between.

If you are single and have no one to provide for in the unfortunate event of your passing, then maybe you don't need life insurance, or at least that much of it. Maybe you need just enough to cover your funeral expenses, if you don't already have that saved, to leave behind for those who will handle your affairs. However, if you have a family who depends on you and your income, your savings, and your effort, then you definitely need life insurance.

Life insurance is exactly what it sounds like—insurance on your life. In case you haven't already guessed, we're about to talk about life insurance in depth now. Stay with me here, because you're gonna want the lowdown. It may protect you and your family.

In the simplest terms, there are two basic types of life insurance—term life and whole life. These sound quite intuitive, and for the most part they are.

Term life insurance is one type of insurance offered by an insurance company to cover the life of an insured over a specified period of time for a specified amount of money. The terms are typically fifteen, twenty, or twenty-five years, and the amounts of coverage, or "face value" of the policy, range from one hundred thousand dollars to more than one million. The cost of this type of policy, or the "premium," is usually affordable since the only benefit provided is a payout in the event of your death. This means that if you die, your insurer pays, and if you do not die by the time the term runs out—congratulations! You didn't die. But the insurance company keeps all the premium you paid unless you have a rider for return of premium (a rider is an add-on benefit). A rider on any form of life insurance will make the premium more expensive because it gives you more options. But straight life insurance pays out the face value of your policy to your beneficiary(ies) if you die within the given term. This type of insurance is meant to cover you during a specific period while you are building wealth, or your nest egg, because the low premiums offer you a safety net while you save and build elsewhere. Many term policies have conversion clauses that allow you to convert the policy at the end of the term to whole life insurance if you would like (for an increased premium, of course). Think of this type of insurance as being like car insurance or homeowners' insurance: if there is no accident, there's no payout. It's also commonly called indemnity insurance.

Whole life insurance is the other type of life insurance offered by an insurance company. Whole life insurance covers the life of the insured for the entirety of his or her lifetime, for a specified amount (again, face value). As long as the premium is paid, the policy guarantees to pay the face value upon the death of the insured. This type of policy has both a pure life insurance coverage benefit and a cash value accumulation benefit. Let me explain. Part of each premium goes to pay for the insurance (just like with term coverage), and the rest accumulates like an investment to provide cash value. This "accumulated cash value" in the policy is invested for greater returns. The cash value will either go into the stock market, as is the case with variable life insurance, or be invested in a fixed rate savings-like account—a guaranteed interest rate that is set when you buy the policy. This is called "cash value whole life insurance." The accumulated cash value can be used by the policyholder as a line of credit or to pay premiums on the policy. If the cash value becomes substantial enough, the policyholder can sometimes use the cash for income in retirement or to pay for premiums without having to pay out of pocket. All these features come with a hefty price tag, however. Whole life insurance is traditionally more than four to five times the cost of term life insurance, depending on the face value of the policy. There are many types of whole life insurance that have different features and benefits, including Universal Life and Variable Universal Life being the most frequently encountered in the marketplace.

All insurance is less expensive when you get it when you are as young and as healthy as possible, so if you are considering it, do not delay! You're not getting any younger. You could get healthier though. If that is your plan, you might want to wait a little and drop a few pounds. Again, just sayin'. You look good though. I'm not judging. Just a tip: insurance companies are all ballbusters. FYI.

The bottom line to remember is that if you need life insurance, then you should get it—but consider your savings habits, your health, and your needs before you purchase a policy. And be sure to shop around. Not all insurance companies are the same. They each target a certain demographic and specialize in specific types of coverage and preferred populations. I'll say it again: shop around and be sure that you're clear on what exactly you are buying.

Regardless of whether you need life insurance, if you depend on your income or you have a family that does, it is imperative that you have disability insurance. If you get sick, are injured, or become incapacitated in some medical way that makes you unable to do your job, you will need income. And unemployment, although nice, will not be anywhere near the income you were used to while you were working. Neither will Social Security Disability Insurance, by the way.

Disability insurance is a type of insurance offered by an insurance company that covers an insured (in other words, you) in the event he or she becomes disabled (as qualified by a doctor). Carriers and policies differ, but standard short-term disability insurance covers you for 66 percent of your pay up to a specified period. Long-term disability insurance usually kicks in after six months of being disabled. Many large employers either provide this coverage or offer it as part of their total health-care package. You can also shop for it on your own in the open market (through an insurance agency). This type of insurance protects against the loss of income in the event of sickness or injury to the insured. According to ssa.gov's Disability Facts, "a 20-year-old has greater than a one-in-four chance of becoming disabled for at least a year before reaching normal retirement age." Disability insurance also covers pregnancy and leave directly following birth as medically necessary. Different policies cover different situations, but know this: disability insurance is important. You cover your car in case of an accident, so why wouldn't you cover your body in the same case?

The challenges that life will inevitably throw at us cannot all be predicted, nor do we want to try to predict them all. We would drive ourselves nuts just trying. We can, however, do our best to somewhat prepare for the very high probability that we will someday be too sick to work, perhaps for an extended period. We may end up in a nursing home or need home health care as we age. There is long-term-care insurance for that. There will be times when we are out of work for prolonged periods, so we need to know what to do and how to lower our expenses and live on less. For every one of life's complications, we can have an answer, that is, if we are diligent, if we are thoughtful, and in some cases, if we have the courage to live a simpler, lighter existence. It's certainly cheaper to live that way.

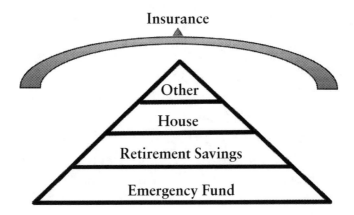

The final piece of our pyramid is what I lump into a category called "Other Investments" or "Other Savings Goals."

You've saved for your emergencies. You've properly funded your retirement savings. You're current on your house payments, and you've protected what you're trying to build. Now you've got some money left over that you want to save for specific, important purposes. "Other investments" or "other savings goals" may be deeply personal. They may be very general. I find that many of these other savings goals fall into several of the following categories:

- college savings accounts
- custodial accounts for children or minors
- special needs trusts
- real estate investment trusts
- brokerage accounts
- stock options
- municipal bonds
- mutual fund accounts
- Christmas Club account
- vacation savings
- rainy day fund
- business interests or partnerships.

Whatever your idea of other savings goals or other investments may be, as long as you are striving to meet your three foundational financial needs, you can call your extra savings whatever you want. You just need to keep in mind the time frame you envision for holding those investments. That time frame is called your **investment time horizon,** also known as the time that you'll hold the asset until you expect to cash it out. The time horizon is very important. It will help you determine how much risk you can reasonably take with that particular asset (pot o' savings).

Assets (or investments, as I defined earlier) are anything that you own that you deem valuable and that can be sold or exchanged for value. If you have an item that someone wants and that person has something that you want, then that item can be seen as valuable or an asset. An asset can be a pot of money (an account) or a rare piece of art, piece of jewelry, coin, collectible, or something of that ilk. An asset can also be a skill that you have that few other people have. These things have value because other people want them. If no one wanted or needed money, there would be no value in it. It's just like if you own a first edition 1960s Barbie doll in mint condition that is still in the box, as opposed to a headless, used 1960s Barbie that everyone has down in the basement somewhere. The two may be the same exact doll, but a lot of people may be interested in buying or exchanging value for the first one because it is rare and therefore desirable. Are you starting to see what I mean by "asset"?

Another point I am making about the term *asset* relates to the next step you should take when creating your financial road map: seek out help and guidance for your financial journey. It's hard to grow your net worth if you don't know what you have in assets and what you owe in liabilities. Financial advisers can help you figure out all that good stuff. You'll find a list of questions to ask when you're ready to find yourself a trustworthy financial adviser in Appendix B at the end of the book.

What Is an Investment Anyway?

I have defined an investment earlier as "any place that you put money and expect it to grow or gain value." That is as simple of a definition as I can conjure. We're going to talk about monetary or financial investments in the next few chapters—what they are and the different types you'll come across—but first we're going to tackle the idea of risk and return. You're going to gain a perspective on investments that you may not have considered before. You're going to read some things that challenge what you thought you knew about investments, and possibly some that you don't like or perhaps don't yet understand. Whatever you glean from this part of the discussion, I assure you, you will learn something new and you'll know what to watch out for when your cousin Fred pitches the next "incredible investment opportunity" to you (no offense to all the good "Cousin Freds" out there!).

Definitions and Misconceptions (How Do I Understand Risk?)

Let's start out with the basics. You invest money with the expectation that it will grow. It will come back bigger than what it was when it went out; otherwise, you would not invest your money at all. You would keep it hidden safely under your mattress. What we need to realize is that not all investments are created equal. They come with a certain level of uncertainty. You may get back less than what you put in or, in the worst-case scenario, get back nothing at all. This is the definition of risk in terms of investments. Risk is the measure of probability that you will get back the money you invested. The higher the degree of uncertainty of loss on the investment, the higher the risk is considered to be. That is why it is so important to understand the relationship between risk and reward with regard to investing your money.

Let me ask you a question that in my view many of my clients answer incorrectly. They do so because of a very common misunderstanding of risk. Answer this question honestly and aloud and do not skip ahead to the answer! I want you to think about it in the context of my prior definition of risk. I want you to think very differently about your money from here on out, so here we go:

You purchase a $1 lottery quick pick every once in a while. Do you see this as a high-risk "investment" or a low-risk "investment"?

I will admit that a $1 purchase seems very negligible in the grand scheme of things, but if you answered that it was low risk because of the relatively low cost of the "investment," you would be wrong. I'll elaborate.

Risk is defined in simple financial terms as the probability that you will get your money back and then some. We all know that one's chance of winning the jackpot for a big-ticket lottery, in the very best odds, is one in twenty-three million. This means that you are very unlikely to get your money back, never mind get more than what you paid in. This is the definition of extremely high risk. You may have clued into my putting the word *investment* in quotation marks as an indication that I do not really view playing the lottery as an investment. It is not. It's a gamble, pure and simple. Gambling is basically throwing money away for entertainment value. The greatest chance of actually getting your money back when gambling, in even the most favorable-odds games such as baccarat and Pai Gow poker, is barely 1 out of 2. Those odds would never be considered an investment in any sound financial plan.

How to Gauge Your Personal Risk Tolerance

Now that I have introduced the concepts of risk and return, let's talk more about what the relative risks and rewards of common types of investments are. This will be an anecdotal discussion, to get your gears turning about how risk and reward work in common investments. In the next chapter, I will provide a full explanation of each type of investment or security (a tradable financial asset). But here I want you to learn about them and gain a realistic expectation of how they can affect your bottom line.

You've likely heard the terms *conservative*, *moderate*, and *aggressive* when discussing different kinds of investments and their relative risks. These are subjective terms, and how they are understood depends on the investor's perception of and comfort with risk, or **risk tolerance**. What I consider to be conservative may not be the same as what you consider to be conservative. It could be that what I consider conservative for my personal portfolio is what you would consider to be aggressive for yours. This all comes back to our individual perception and comfort level with the possibility that we could lose money. Of course, in the end, no one wants to lose money. That is a given, but it is hardly ever achievable. There may be pros and cons to losing money and to gaining it. Let's dig in to this idea a bit.

Many people, not understanding the concept of risk tolerance, oftentimes see their own risk tolerance changing with the whims of the market. Your risk tolerance should *not change with the market* but, instead, should change with your **time horizon**. Your time horizon is the time period you have until you take out or use the money you have invested. If you have only a little bit of time, say, less than three years, then you should not invest your money in a vehicle with a high probability of fluctuating in value, because there is a reasonable chance that your investment could be worth less than what you put in when you go to use it. The funny thing about investment risk is that it tends to dwindle the longer you hold the investment as part of a well-diversified **portfolio**. Encouraging you to have a diversified portfolio is a fancy way of saying, "Don't put all your eggs in one basket." You've surely heard that before. When you have so much money that you are able to invest, that is called your "portfolio." We *diversify*, or spread out our money, to mitigate the risk that any one of our investments won't pan out the way we'd hoped or to be sure to take advantage of all the opportunities that the markets have to offer. Of course, diversification doesn't ensure a profit or protect against loss.

There are several investment markets available to you at any given time. For instance, you have the stock market, which covers stocks, stock mutual funds, preferred stocks, and stock options. You also have the bond market, which covers corporate bonds, convertible bonds, government bonds, municipal bonds, and bond mutual funds. Then you have the real estate market, which covers real property, either commercial or residential. These three major markets are not the only markets that exist— there is a market for practically every investment known to humankind—but they are the three I am going to focus on to keep things relatively simple for our discussion. They are utilized most commonly among investors like you and me. I'd like to illustrate how markets and diversification work so that you will clearly understand what I mean when I use these terms again throughout the rest of *Money Moves*, because they'll come up a lot. I'm going to use real estate in this primary example because most people can easily relate to that market. Many are under the misconception that real estate is a sure thing, but it has its risks like any other investment type.

Let's suppose that you are in the market to buy a new house. You contact your realtor to find a list of homes that fit your ideal criteria for location, price, number of bedrooms, type of yard, etc. You then go out and look for the perfect house. You are not willing or able at this time to pay more than a certain price for this house, let's say $200,000. Your realtor shows you a few houses in your desired area, and a few more just outside that location to give you alternative options. She tells you that inventory in your preferred neighborhood is very low at this time (meaning there are not many homes available for purchase) and that the few being sold are going fast.

This is an example of the market, or the supply of houses in relation to the demand for that particular neighborhood. Conversely, if there are many houses available to buy and very few buyers in the market, there is more inventory than there are buyers. This is referred to as a **buyer's market**. In this market, the buyer has the opportunity to negotiate with multiple sellers to get a better deal because the supply of available houses is greater than the number of interested buyers. This drives the prices down and the overall market down too.

In the first example, it is a **seller's market**. In this market, the seller has the advantage because there are fewer available homes than there are buyers who want to purchase. The sellers have the opportunity to negotiate for a higher price because of the lack of purchase options in the marketplace. Buyers will be willing to pay more to get what they want. This drives the prices and the overall market up. Let's explore the example a bit further.

Your realtor takes you to the homes in your ideal neighborhood. You find them to be all right, but not the perfect fit for you. You love the area—the neighborhood is clean and has good schools and low crime—but the homes do not fit your ideal. You decide that $200,000 is a lot of money to spend if you are not completely satisfied, so you agree to go with your realtor to the outside neighborhoods and explore the options there. You find passable homes, but nothing enticing enough to draw you away from your desired neighborhood. So, what are your options at this juncture?

You could negotiate with the sellers of the available homes in the area you want, or you could opt not to buy anything at this particular time and wait for a break in the market. You may find either that the sellers are not willing to negotiate or that you can't afford to wait because you need somewhere to live and are against renting in the current economic environment. You may also believe that the market is still on its way up and that now is the right time for you to purchase a home. But whatever your view of the current market, the available options, and the overall direction of the economy, you have to make some assumptions about the risk of the proposed investment. You have to consider the diversifiable and systematic risks of buying that house.

Diversifiable risk is risk that can be reduced or eliminated through diversification. Diversification is just what it sounds like, the idea that you create diversity among your investments by putting your money in different places. This creates balance. You may have heard this another way as "Don't put all your eggs in one basket" like I've said before. If that one basket drops, bye-bye breakfast. Diversifiable risk is also sometimes referred to as single-asset or sector risk because your investment is only in one place (one asset or one market). In the foregoing example, instead of spending your entire $200,000 on one house in one area, you could buy two or three smaller houses in different areas to spread out the risk that one of the houses might become less desirable in the future. You can mitigate the risk of losing value on your home if you end up with neighbors who paint their houses shocking lime green or do not keep up with the maintenance of their properties, thus affecting the salability of your home in the future. If you buy more than one asset, or more than one house in this case, you have a greater chance that at least one of them will make up the gains for the others in your portfolio. This is just a simple example. Not many people do this with houses, by the way.

Systematic risk, on the other hand, is risk that cannot be reduced or eliminated through diversification; it is essentially beyond investor control. Systematic risk is sometimes referred to as market or economic risk because it is the inherent risk that comes with participating in any given financial environment. If the overall housing market is low or the overall economy is low, you can't do much else about that systematic risk but wait it out. These two types of risk exist for investments of all asset classes and types.

Now back to our example. Knowing that it may be a risk to miss out on buying in a down market, you act on your gut instinct and try negotiating with the sellers in your ideal neighborhood.

Your negotiations are less than ideal but somewhat successful, so you decide to go ahead and buy one of the houses in your desired neighborhood. You think the market is relatively low and that its value will go up in the near future. You agree to an offer of $205,000 for a two-bedroom, two-bathroom house with a nice yard and a one-car garage. You are content with your purchase despite having gone a little over your budget and settling for one bedroom less than you would have preferred. Although $205,000 was a bit more than you thought you could afford, you believe you can still make it work with a combination of cash down and a mortgage to make up the rest. You have a preapproval letter from the bank for $200,000 at the prime interest rate, but you are sure you can get the rest covered with a slightly higher interest rate through the bank.

In the back of your mind, you are a little concerned about the price and your ability to make the monthly mortgage payments, but you hope that the market will go up soon and you will be able to refinance at a lower interest rate in the near future. The risk that you will not be able to make your mortgage payments and thus face foreclosure and seizure of your property by the bank is called **default risk.** Usually we talk about default risk when an investor is loaning out money and will collect interest until the loan is repaid. This is typically the case when one uses bonds in one's portfolio, but it is very much the same when a bank loans you money and expects you to pay it back. The bank is assuming the default risk on you (their investment) through the issuance of the mortgage. If you don't pay back your loan—in other words, if you default—the bank can claim ownership of the collateral you used to get the loan (your house), leaving you with no asset and bad credit. This is another example of the risk associated with buying and selling investments.

Everything into which we invest money has inherent risk, even that which is deemed riskless. A **riskless asset** is typically one issued by the US government, such as a treasury security. The reason it is called a riskless investment is because the government can essentially print more money to pay you back, and there is hardly a country on earth with more economic stability than the United States. Despite what political pundits may discuss, the US government issues notes (currency, cash money, T-bills) that are extremely likely to be paid back. I would caution you, though: do not believe that a riskless asset is truly without any risk. As I have mentioned before, there are a great many risks that exist in the investing world, and one to be aware of is **inflation risk**.

Inflation is the economic effect that causes all your expenses to go up over time. Therefore, inflation risk is the risk that your investment will not increase in value at a greater rate than the costs of everyday living. If your expenses go up over time and your investments or assets don't appreciate in kind, your investments end up being worth less than when you acquired them. Looking at it in this way, you are in fact losing money on your investments, because if you were to sell them or cash them in, you would not be able to buy the same quantity of things as you were able to buy previously. You lose purchasing power, and thus you lose money. Inflation risk is often overlooked by the average investor, but I will illustrate how it is a very real and very powerful risk that you must overcome to keep your investments sound.

Suppose it's 1982 and you have $10,000. The oil embargo

has recently ended, the housing market is turning around, you are hearing good things about bonds, and interest rates are high. You are a bit skittish about stocks because your friend Larry has a cousin Darryl who lost his shirt after investing because of a stock tip from his boss's broker. So, you decide to put your money into your local credit union and benefit from their advertised 8 percent interest on a standard savings account. You're as happy as a clam and collecting a nice bit of interest. This goes on for years. You don't even bother checking the account; you simply file your statements as they come in.

Fast-forward fifteen years. Unbeknownst to you, your credit union changed the interest rate on your savings account several times, and now, in 1997, that cushy 8 percent interest rate has dwindled to a measly 2 percent. Meanwhile, inflation over those fifteen years has averaged 3.2 percent. Now your account is earning 1.2 percent less than the rate of inflation. What does that mean?

It means that your money is not growing as fast as your everyday expenses. It's costing you more and more to live while your money is making less and less. Remember back in 1982 when a stamp cost twenty cents? Now imagine it's 1997 and that same stamp costs you thirty-two cents. That is a 60 percent increase in the cost of that stamp over a fifteen-year period! That means that everything in your life is becoming increasingly more expensive through no fault of your own. To ensure that you can continue to enjoy the same standard of living, you have to make sure your money is invested so that it keeps up with the mystical power of inflation. Otherwise, you can say goodbye to those Z Cavaricci's and Hypercolor shirts because you can't afford them!

Inflation risk, diversifiable risk, market risk, default risk, risk, risk, risk, risk … what does it all mean? It means that there is nowhere on earth that you can put your money that doesn't involve some possibility of loss. You might say, "I can put my money in a box under my bed." I would say, "What if your house burns down?" You might say, "I'll invest in a chateau in France," and I would say, "What if the franc depreciates or there's an earthquake?" Every investment known to humankind has risk. It's a fact of life. It's a factor of doing business, or of not doing business, but the bottom line is that there is risk in everything you do. There is risk when you walk out your front door of being struck by lightning. The risk exists. Knowing the probability of the negative outcome of the risks that you decide to take on is the key to investing wisely. You must determine your own personal comfort level with risk.

When considering an investment, you should ask yourself the following five simple questions:

1. "What types of risks could affect my money?"
2. "Do I understand how my money is invested and how it could potentially grow?"
3. "Do I feel comfortable (that is, could I sleep at night?) knowing that my money could be worth less than what I put in at any given time?"
4. "What would I do if the market for this particular investment were to suddenly drop significantly (say, by 15 percent)?"
5. "Within what time frame do I expect to use or need to use this money?"

As I mentioned before, the longer you have to hold on to a particular asset, the more the risk tends to diminish. This is not true of every investment; however, it is typically true of a well-diversified portfolio of investments aggregated to achieve a specific objective. Ask yourself also, "What is my goal with this money?" If it's to get rich overnight, either you have your expectation of reasonable return way out of whack, or you're just plain gambling.

Here I'll outline a reasonable rate of return, align it to its corresponding risk, and explain it so that you can apply your own ideas about investments. Remember what I said, however:

there are no sure things. There are only calculated risks, time, and the added help of diversification. The easiest and most surefire way to get rich is to invest a lot of money over a long period of time while keeping expenses low and not touching your nest egg. If you can do that, you will gain wealth.

Relative Measures of Risk

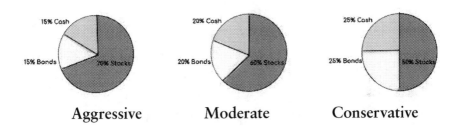

| Aggressive | Moderate | Conservative |

In general terms, if you are an **aggressive investor**, you are typically marked by three characteristics:

1. You have a long-term time horizon.
   You can afford to wait and to withstand short-term market fluctuations. Since you aren't pressed for time with your investment, you are able to wait out a market downturn that may decrease the value of your portfolio temporarily. Long term would generally be defined as ten years or longer.

2. Your ability to stomach the peaks and valleys of the stock markets (and sometimes bond or real estate markets).
   Everyone can stomach the ups, but can you stay put and keep your money invested when values decrease? Even better, could you recognize the buying opportunity of discounted prices on those same assets?

3. You have emergency money that is easily accessible to cover your short-term needs. If you don't have emergency

funds available, then taking on extra risk is not advisable. You could lose your job or become ill, or your roof could start leaking. It's important to have money in reserve before you decide to invest aggressively.

An aggressive portfolio is typically one where the majority of your money is invested in the stock market. The stock market is presumed to be more volatile than the bond or real estate markets and generally is thought to be riskier as calculated by these measures. The truth is, stock prices do historically fluctuate at a much faster rate than either bond or real estate prices do, and because of this, they carry more risk. This is because at any given moment, the price of the stock could, and likely will, be different from when you purchased it. I think of an aggressive portfolio as one in which greater than 70 percent of the assets is in stocks. Is that necessarily a bad thing? No. It just means that you should know the relative risk and the rate of return that you can expect to see in your portfolio. An aggressive portfolio with 70 percent invested in diversified stocks, 15 percent invested in diversified bonds, and 15 percent being in cash or cash equivalents should reasonably expect a higher-than-average rate of return for the increased risk of being more heavily weighted in the stock market.

Now, using a much higher-than-average assumed rate of return for all years in a portfolio is a fatal error in financial planning. It is much wiser to assume a lower rate of return and plan for slower growth of the portfolio than to overestimate and come up short. If you plan for a 9 percent rate of return over twenty years and it turns out you actually achieved 10 percent, then you are delighted that you have more money than you anticipated. On the flip side, if you plan for a 10 percent rate of return and your portfolio only achieves 9 percent, then you are either stuck waiting for your money to grow to that anticipated number or upset that your money didn't grow as expected. This can be disastrous, particularly for retirement planning purposes. People are typically happier when they find they can retire earlier, and they're typically angrier when they wake up and find that they have to wait because their assumptions were flawed. Seems like common sense would help people avoid this, but I have seen it happen time and time again. I know a 1 percent difference in the average annual rate of return seems negligible, but believe me, when we're talking about compounding interest over a twenty-year period, the money really adds up! This is why it's also important to consider the fees you are paying on your portfolio as well as the relative risk. We will discuss the breakdown and importance of fees later on. One step at a time.

A **moderate investor** is one who is uncomfortable being aggressive but realizes that a conservative approach will either take too long or require too much upfront investment. A moderate investor can have a shorter-term time horizon, but this will be no less than five to seven years until she needs to start using her money. She also enjoys just getting a moderate rate of return, middle of the road: not too much risk, not too little return. This type of investor typically just wants to make what the market will offer, a reasonable rate of return on a moderate portfolio should track with the general markets' average annual return. She will have about 60 percent of her money invested in stocks, with the remaining 40 percent divided among fixed income assets (bonds and cash). She will also have some money saved; however, because she has a good portion of her portfolio in cash, she may feel okay dipping into just that portion from time to time to cover special needs.

Finally, **conservative investors** will either have a shorter time frame in which to invest money or a serious fear of losing money at any given moment—or both. These investors can be of any age and may have any level of sophistication to their understanding of investments. The bottom line is, they just can't stomach the possibility of losing money or they can't get their heads around how investments work. That is perfectly okay. These types of investors need to know that their money is relatively stable and that although it will earn less over time, it will bounce around in the market a lot less as well. A reasonable rate of assumed return will be below what the typical market rates average annually. The conservative investor's portfolio will be made up of 50 percent or less in stock holdings and 50 percent or more in fixed income assets.

I keep using the phrase *average annual return*. Some years you may make 8 percent, and some years you may earn 12 percent. The average annual return is calculated by adding your actual return for each year and dividing that total by the number of years you have held the investment. Here's an example:

Sally has a well-diversified portfolio of mutual funds. She has held them for the past ten years and considers herself to be a moderate investor. Her effective rates of return for each of the past ten years were as follows:

2006: 16%	2010: 4%	2014: 13%
2007: 15%	2011: 12%	2015: 9%
2008: –10%	2012: 11%	
2009: 2%	2013: 10%	

If you add all these numbers up, you get eighty-two. When you divide eighty-two by ten years, you get an average annual return of 8.2 percent. Not too shabby for a moderate portfolio.

If you ever hear anyone tell you they achieved high double-digit returns over an extended period of time, be very skeptical. It is unlikely in any type of mainstream investment that someone would consistently achieve high double digits for any length of time. You should be aware that promised returns above 5 percent or 6 percent across an extended period of time must involve considerable risk. Ask yourself, and perhaps the person telling you about this allegedly hot investment tip, "What's the catch?" There always is one.

If you hear about incredibly attractive rates of return given a certain prevailing interest rate environment (think about how the banks are paying a pitiful 1 percent on deposits right now), ask some important questions before you even consider investing, such as the following:

- What do I have to give up to get that interest rate? Typically, the answer will be liquidity. You'll have to leave the money in the investment for a certain period of time, and you may be penalized for taking money out early.
- What types of risks are involved in this particular investment?
- Is the interest rate guaranteed or backed by any insurance, government, or contract? Is the interest rate flexible, or does it cover a specified period? (Is this a teaser rate?)
- When and how can I take out the money?

Oftentimes, especially in today's terms, these attractive interest rates are part of a rider, or addendum, on a security called a "variable annuity," which is a type of vehicle that you can invest in for retirement. Attractive interest rates aren't necessarily a bad thing, but you should know if you're getting into a variable annuity and all the bells and whistles that go along with it before you sign the contract. Annuities are somewhat complex insurance products that we will discuss at length. They're not products designed for wealth accumulation, but they do have value for those seeking a guaranteed payment at retirement. Look to chapter 9 for further discussion on variable annuities.

Regardless of your risk tolerance, you should consider investing your hard-earned money so that it's working as hard as you are to make you wealthy. You should also be aware of the risks and rewards associated with the many types of investment products and vehicles out there. Some are better than others, but your particular portfolio of investments should be tailored to your specific interests and desires, just like your financial plan. In the end, if you're saving money, you're doing the right thing. Just remember, the higher the assumed rate of interest, the higher the risk involved. Said another way, the lower the risk you are willing to take to achieve your financial goals, the greater the investment you will have to make to reach those goals. The money has to come from somewhere, so if you're earning lower interest, you have to invest more. If you don't have much to invest but you have a long time to save, you may be able to take on more risk to achieve higher returns to get you there. Risk and return are generally directly correlated.

Common Investment Securities to Know About

Let's talk now about some of the most common types of investments and what they could mean to you and your portfolio. Here we'll cover the ins and outs of stocks, bonds, and mutual funds. I'll talk about the markets for each, how to buy and sell these products, what to look for, and what to avoid. We'll also discuss how you can give yourself an edge for one day achieving your wealth goals. Let's get to it. You ready?! You can do this!

Stocks

What is a stock? In plain English, it is a tiny piece of ownership in a company. The more shares of stock you own of a particular company, the more ownership rights you have over that company. If you end up buying more than 50 percent of the outstanding stocks in a particular company, then you are said to have a controlling interest in that company.

When a company is "born," meaning an organization becomes "incorporated," stock shares are created. Those stock shares are owned by the original investors or owners of the company, typically the founders who invested their time, money, and blood, sweat, and tears into making it a viable business. Since you are purchasing ownership in a company when you purchase a stock, you are said to have **equity** in the company. That is why a stock is referred to as an "equity asset." You may hear people on TV talking about investment in equities. They're talking about stock securities.

As a shareholder of a company, you are also an owner. If a company goes belly up, the owners have the last claim to the assets left over. If a company performs exceptionally well, the shareholders have unlimited growth potential.

Companies can be either publicly or privately held. If a company is public, it means that the company's stock shares are available for purchase by the general public. A private company has stock shares, but they are owned by a private group of people, and the shares are not available for purchase by the general public. Coca-Cola is an example of a public company. Publix Super Markets is an example of a private company. Go ahead, double-check me. Google "Coca-Cola stock shares." You will see a page pop up with the symbol, also known as a **ticker** symbol, "KO." A ticker symbol is simply the identifier for a specific company within the stock market. At the top of the page, the **quote** looks like this:

> The Coca-Cola Company
> NYSE: KO—December 20, 4:05 p.m. EST
> 41.66 USD price decrease 0.01 (0.02%)

This quote, or stock quote, tells you the price ($41.66), the date and time (December 20, 4:05 p.m. Eastern Standard Time), the exchange on which the stock is traded (NYSE, or New York Stock Exchange), and the price change for the day. The exchange is the place where the stock is bought and sold—in other words, the market. This is how the stock market works. There are several exchanges where different stocks are traded, depending on many factors such as price, size, industry, location, and type of company. For example, most US stocks are sold on the New York Stock Exchange (NYSE) and the NASDAQ (a funny name that once stood for National Association of Securities Dealers Automated Quotations), whereas you'll find Japanese companies trading on the Tokyo Stock Exchange.

The market for a particular stock, or the ability to buy and sell the stock, will depend on the supply from sellers and the demand from buyers. Just like it is in the real estate world for houses, if there are many stocks for sale in a particular market but not many buyers, the prices of the stocks are likely to go down. If there are many people who want to sell shares in a particular company, say, KO (Coca-Cola), but not many who want to buy any, the price of Coca-Cola is likely to go down. If the reverse is true and there are many people willing to buy KO but not many willing to sell, the price of the stock will likely go up. Unlike the housing market, the stock market moves very quickly, and therefore the prices of stocks change rapidly. If you were to watch a stock's price change throughout the day, you would see changes nearly every second. What you are viewing is the movement of shares between buyers and sellers throughout the day. People can't buy and sell houses multiple times in a day, so the prices of houses don't change as rapidly as the prices for stocks. But fundamentally the markets work the same way. Buyers and sellers come together to exchange shares and money. Changes in stock prices throughout the day are simply evidence of activity in the market.

Now, google Publix Super Markets stock. You won't find a stock quote. The shares are not publicly held and not listed on a stock exchange and therefore are not available for purchase by the general public. They are only available for purchase through private transactions. The popular southeast US grocery store chain Publix is actually entirely owned by its employees and board of directors. A phrase we use for this idea is *wholly owned.*

Historically, stocks have returned an average of 11 percent

since 1926. Their prices ebb and flow with other economic factors. This is an aggregate average, meaning that if you had invested in every company listed in the public stock market since 1926, you would have seen an average annual return of about 11 percent in your portfolio. Your portfolio would have been made up of thousands of different companies. The holdings in your portfolio (the total of your invested assets) would have risen and fallen regularly over that long period of time. Of course, some companies would have gone out of business, or "gone to zero." This means that the stock would be worthless; it would have a price of $0. Other companies would have been "born" and grown at incredible rates to compensate for the ones that went kaput.

Picking a company to invest in has its risks. You could pick a company that grows at lightning speed. You could pick one that barely grows at all. How do you know what to pick? You will know when you understand how the company makes money, what your risk tolerance is, and how many different companies you can afford to buy. The key to mitigating the risk that a single company may go out of business and therefore cause you to lose money within your portfolio is **diversification**. Remember, diversification means not putting all your eggs into one basket. It means that instead of investing your money in only a small number of stocks in a limited number of industries, you spread your money out over several different companies and across several different unrelated industries. Here's an example:

You have one thousand dollars to invest. You have many options of different stocks that you might be interested in buying. You make a list of companies across five major industries that you think have quality goods, quality services, and business practices that align with your ideals and values. The list looks like this (this is a random list and not an endorsement of any company or stock pick. It's just a simple example with well-known companies):

Technology	Financials	Energy	Consumer goods	Healthcare
Apple, Inc.	Chase	Exxon	Target	HCA
Microsoft	Citibank	Sunoco	Coach	Tenet
Facebook	MetLife	FPL	Whole Foods	Eli Lilly
IBM	Prudential	BP	Home Depot	GSK

With one thousand dollars, you could opt to purchase almost six shares of Apple Inc. or twenty-one shares of GSK (GlaxoSmithKline), but either of those options would leave you subject to the performance of just one company's stock within one industry. What would happen if the company's management suddenly became ineffectual? What if they were to make a wrong turn in their business process that results in decreased sales or some other major hiccup in growth? What if the industry as a whole goes through a slump? You can avoid those individual company and industry risks by investing in many different companies and industries simultaneously. Instead of concentrating all your money into a few companies, according to modern portfolio theory, you should buy between ten and twelve different companies of varying sizes and from varied industries to achieve optimal diversification in your portfolio.

In addition to diversifying your stock portfolio, you further reduce risk by investing in different types of assets that can provide balance to your overall portfolio when the stock market as a whole is not so attractive. Stocks and bonds, although not the only available investments in the universe, are the most common. They are referred to as securities. There's that word again. Remember, I briefly defined a security as a tradable financial asset, but to give you a more thorough idea, let's look at *Merriam-Webster*'s definition of a security: "an instrument of investment in the form of a document (as a stock certificate or bond) providing evidence of its ownership." Let's move on to bonds then, shall we?

Bonds

Unlike with a stock share, when you purchase a bond, you don't actually own anything. A bond is like an IOU that a company or government issues to you in exchange for your cash. You loan money to that company or government, and they promise to pay you back with interest over a specific period of time. Therefore, when you hold bonds, you are a creditor of the issuer.

As with a stock, a company will issue bonds when they need to raise capital for different projects or strategic plans that drive growth. The company or government owes you your money back. This creates a debt for the company and a credit for you, the investor. This is why a bond is referred to as a "debt instrument." Bonds are also known as **fixed income assets** because historically they paid one fixed interest rate. Nowadays, variable rates are more common, as is the case with bond mutual funds and the like.

So, how does a bond work? A bondholder (you) lends a specific amount of money to a company or government, usually in multiples of one thousand dollars. This is known as the initial price or **face value** of the bond. The bond issuer (the company or government) states the time period of the bond, known as the **maturity date**. This is the date when you can expect to get your loan back. The issuer tells you the interest rate they will pay on the loan, also known as the **coupon rate**. The coupon is the return you earn for loaning out your money. It is usually paid once or twice a year. And finally, the bond states the amount of requested debt or the **total outstanding bond issue**. This is the amount the company or government feels would be required to complete the desired project or initiative.

Some bond issues are long term, and some are short term. For example, the US government routinely sells bonds that mature over thirty years or more. Other municipalities may issue five- or ten-year bonds for specific infrastructure projects such as roads or bridges. These bonds are repaid within a much shorter time period, relative to when the project that the bond financed is completed.

For a creditor, the risks involved in owning bonds are the default risk and the interest rate risk. As we discussed, default risk is the possibility that the issuer won't be able to pay back the loan. One way to assess whether a bond issuer is likely to pay back a loan is through independent rating services such as Moody's, Fitch Ratings, AM Best, and Standard & Poor's. Bonds rated AAA are the most likely to be paid back and thus will have comparatively lower interest payments. The higher the risk that an issuer will not pay back the loan, the higher the interest rate will be. The interest rate has to be high enough to incentivize an investor to take on that additional risk. That's the risk–return trade-off. Bonds rated BB or lower are considered junk or high-yield bonds and hold higher rates of risk as well as higher rates of return.

Interest rate risks affect bonds in significant ways. When interest rates go up in the marketplace, outstanding bonds become less attractive. Would you want to hold onto a lower-interest-yielding bond when a new one promises a higher rate? Probably not. So, to get rid of the bond, you have to sell it in the same market where new bonds promise higher rates. To do this, you need an incentive. The incentive is to lower the price of your bond to less than the face value.

Let me give you an example: Let's say you buy a Miami-Dade County municipal bond today with a maturity date of December 31, 2026, and a coupon rate of 4 percent. That means for every thousand dollars you invest, you will receive an annual payment of forty dollars (4% of $1,000) until the bond is repaid on December 31, 2026.

Prevailing interest rates in today's market are very low when compared to historical rates. Let's say that next year, the Federal Reserve decides to raise interest rates, which then results in new Miami-Dade County municipal bonds being issued with a coupon rate of 5 percent. What does that mean for you? In one short twelve-month period, the bonds you're holding have become less attractive to the marketplace. You may be asking yourself, "But why?" Because if you were to sell your bonds in the market, you would not have any buyers willing to pay full price for 4 percent bonds, when they can simply go to the bond issuer (Miami-Dade County) and buy new bonds that pay a higher interest rate (5 percent). That means that if you want to sell your bonds, you will have to do something to make the idea more attractive to a buyer. What would you do?

You have two options:

1. Keep the bonds you have, and be content with the 4 percent interest rate you enjoy, either until maturity or until interest rates become more favorable for you to sell.
2. Lower your price for the bonds in order to compensate the buyer for the reduction in interest rate payment.

What does the above example tell us about the relationship between interest rates and bond prices? As interest rates go up, bond prices go down. Also, the reverse is true: as interest rates go down, bond prices go up. It's not the face value of the bond that goes up, but the price that you could resell it for in the marketplace. This is because the original interest rate you were promised is higher than the prevailing market interest rate, which makes the bond more valuable overall. This means that bond prices have an **inverse relationship** to interest rates.

Let me give you another example of a more common type of bond with which you may have a little more experience, US savings bonds. When I was a kid, without fail, every birthday, special occasion, and Christmas my grandparents, who were Depression-era kids themselves, gave all their grandchildren fifty-dollar US government savings bonds. Yes, as our gifts. I am not ungrateful, but I will give a word of caution: don't expect a whole lot of hoopla from a six-year-old when he or she opens a card with a multicolored piece of paper that has a bit of fancy writing and a big 5-0 printed on the top.

I look back now and think of how smart my grandparents were to give us those bonds. I think fondly about the concern they must have had for our future when they purchased the lot of them (I have a couple of siblings and a great many cousins in my family). As we got older, the denominations grew larger as well. The money was meant to give us a boost for college. I think by the time I graduated high school I had amassed two thousand dollars' worth or so in US savings bonds. Of course, I didn't fully understand what that meant and I wasn't sure what exactly I would use them for, but I did realize eventually that my grandparents were just about the only people in the world who were actively thinking about setting up my financial future.

So how do US savings bonds work? Let me tell you a little story. Personally, I had no clue, but I was about to find out. You know how sometimes you learn things through books, and sometimes from the experiences of others, and other times by doing things the hard way? This was one of those "doing things the hard way" times.

I was already well into my junior year at Florida State University, living in my own apartment, working for a living, and loving life. One day, I had packed up some stuff to take to Goodwill. As I started backing out of my parking space, although I had looked back through my rearview mirror before lifting off the brake, I didn't see the low-riding purple Honda Civic trying to skirt around me. I surely wasn't going five miles per hour, but I backed into the driver's car hard enough that it seemed to dent her hood and scratch the front end something awful. Needless to say, she was angry. I immediately jumped out of the car and apologized for not having seen her, thinking a million things at once, but never even contemplating calling the police. That was my first mistake. Suffice it to say that I made an avalanche of mistakes from there, culminating in my US savings bond lesson.

Next, I showed no hesitation in taking the blame (mistake #2) and vowed to repair her car no matter what (mistake #3). I'm not saying that one should shirk responsibility when one has made a mistake, but this was clearly an accident. I have since learned that there are many factors to consider and that the first thing to do is call the authorities.

But this was my first "major" accident, causing adrenaline to pump through my veins, and that day I learned many lessons the hard way. What does this have to do with my savings bonds, you say? Well, since they were the only major "extra" savings I had to my name, I thought I could just cash them in, fix the woman's car, and be done with it. After all, it seemed like the right thing to do.

The other driver and I exchanged information. I told her I would take care of the damage to her car and that she should just go get an estimate for the repairs (mistake #4). She came back the next day with a written estimate of thirteen hundred dollars (please remember that this was 1998). I was floored! I told her I needed some time to get the money together. I thought hard about what I could do to avoid using up the majority of my nest egg to cover this one accident. I certainly couldn't call my mother! She would kill me! I thought to myself, *You are an independent, responsible woman. You did this. Now you have to suffer the consequences.* So, I took my two thousand dollars' worth of US savings bonds down to the local bank and asked to cash them out. Of course, what I neglected to consider was that not all the bonds had fully matured to face value.

And this, friends, was my first hard lesson in the bond market. I thought I had two thousand dollars in savings, but unbeknownst to me, the bonds needed time to mature to their full value (try about thirty years these days!). US savings bonds are known as **zero-coupon** bonds because instead of their paying out a percentage of interest each year, the buyer invests only a portion of the face value and waits for the bond to mature to the full value stated on the bond itself.

You can see where this is going. Some of the bonds, such as those I received when I was born, nineteen years prior, were actually worth what was printed on the fancy paper. The others were worth somewhere between half and full face value depending on their age. What I failed to understand was that when my grandparents purchased the bonds, they didn't pay the full fifty dollars for them at the time of purchase. They paid half—and the interest that accrued until the maturity date would bring the face value to the full fifty dollars at the date stated on the bond. Crazy, right?! Not really. I just didn't know how they worked. So, I ended up leaving the bank that day with a little more than one thousand four hundred fifty dollars (biggest mistake of all!) and a terribly bruised ego. I felt pretty dumb. I may have even raised a fuss at the bank. Poor teller woman.

Anyway, I went back to the woman with the purple Civic and, yep, you guessed it, cut her a friggin' check for $1,300. Luckily, she had her car repaired within a week, so I know she didn't pocket my savings—well, at least not all of it. Let's just say my mother ripped me a new one when she found out what I had done. I thought I was going to make her so proud for doing the "right" thing! She was proud that I took responsibility, but as for everything else, she made sure I understood that I must never do that again!

I have not forgotten those important lessons, and I learned firsthand how government bonds really work. The moral of the story? Sometimes when you make a great many mistakes and you learn from them, the lesson really sticks! All in all, I think it was a good investment with relatively little sustained loss, save my bruised ego.

Now that you have a basic understanding of stocks and bonds, let's talk about other investment vehicles that offer additional options for your portfolio and provide more diversification to help you achieve your long- and short-term financial goals.

Mutual Funds

In the first two sections of this chapter, I laid a foundation for your understanding of the simplest investment securities. With that information in mind, we can now build a view of the world of investments. If you didn't understand what a stock or a bond was or how they work, then it might be hard for you to understand mutual funds. That's because mutual funds are made up of stocks and bonds as well as other investment vehicles. You may have some familiarity with mutual funds from any 401(k) investments you have. Let's break it down.

Think of a **mutual fund** as a sort of investment basket with a stated overall goal called an "investment objective." There is a manager of the basket (either an individual or a team of managers who work together for a mutual fund company) who chooses what will be allowed in the basket based on the fund's objective. The basket will contain investment assets such as stocks, bonds, and cash that together combine to achieve the mutual fund **objective**.

Some examples of investment objectives listed in order from higher to lower risk are:

Maximum capital appreciation
Growth
Value
Growth and Income
Income
Capital Preservation

Each investment objective can be tied to a person's risk tolerance or time horizon—or both. For example, a younger investor who is not risk-averse may be more likely to invest in a fund with maximum capital appreciation as its objective because she wants to grow her money as much as possible in the time she has available. She has a long time period until the money will be used for retirement, so she can afford to withstand the ups and downs of the market with a riskier fund that seeks higher growth.

On the other hand, an older investor may not have very long until she needs to use her money. She may seek to preserve what she has worked so hard to save. Therefore, a fund with the objective of preservation of capital, like a money market mutual fund, could be the right choice for her. This type of fund is less volatile and has less money invested in assets that have the possibility for large price fluctuations. Typical investments in these funds, such as certificates of deposit, money market mutual funds, and government bonds, are common. I will add that mutual funds, regardless of their risk profile, are not FDIC insured or guaranteed by any agency or company. They are completely reliant on the performance of the underlying investments in which the fund invests. The fund is simply a gathering of money that is divided up among different assets in order to achieve a stated objective. The success of the vehicle is determined by the manager's ability to choose and invest in assets that line up with the fund's objective. These are only examples. Investors of all ages have different time horizons and different risk tolerances that should be carefully considered prior to investing any money.

After the investment objective is set for the fund, the manager establishes the fund's investment **style**. The investment style provides a specific prescription for the types of assets that will make up the components of the fund. Types of assets common in mutual funds are as follows:

- domestic large company (large cap or large capitalization) stock
- domestic medium company (midcap or mid capitalization) stock
- domestic small company (small cap or small capitalization) stock

- international company stock
- real estate investment (real estate investment trust fund, or REIT)
- domestic government bonds
- international government bonds
- domestic corporate bonds
- international corporate bonds
- domestic high-yield bonds
- international high-yield bonds
- microcap stock (very small company stock)
- emerging markets stock (stock of companies from other countries with emerging market economies)

The mutual fund basket will be filled with assets that meet the criteria for both the fund objective and the fund style. Each investor in the fund pools his or her money in the basket, and in exchange, the manager gives all the investors access to the assets that will satisfy the investment objective and the style and that they believe will most likely achieve the goals of the fund. By pooling money in the basket, individual investors can achieve the all-important objective of diversification without having to buy individual assets on their own. The money is pooled with that of other like investors to provide access to higher-quality diversified investments. The fund is then broken up into shares and allocated to each investor as a shareholder in the fund according to the investment amount of each. To better visualize this, imagine that I have ten thousand dollars and I want to invest in the XYZ Large-Cap Mutual Fund. Each share of the fund is priced at ten dollars, so if I invest the full ten thousand dollars, I will receive one thousand shares of that fund.

Mutual funds typically require an initial minimum amount of money to buy into the fund. There are also restrictions on trading in and out of mutual funds as they are long-term investment vehicles. Short-term trading in mutual funds hurts the long-term buy-and-hold nature of the portfolio.

You must be thinking, *How do I know which mutual fund to choose?* Well, you'll need to figure out a few things about yourself before you decide. Here's a handy checklist to help you navigate the business of choosing a mutual fund as part of your investment portfolio:

____ Do I know the investment objective I am trying to achieve with my money?

____ Do I know how long I will want to keep the money invested?

____ Do I have an aversion to certain types of risk?

____ Is there a particular sector of business that I want to avoid?

____ Is there a particular sector of business that I want to seek out?

____ Am I ready to make an investment decision right now?

____ Do I have enough money to exceed the minimums for the funds in which I am looking to invest?

When searching for a mutual fund that fits your needs based on your answers to these questions, you will first screen for the funds that align with your overall objective, criteria, time horizon, and current investable assets. Let's take a look at how you might go about that.

Many brokerage firms have a stock or mutual fund screener tool built into their online hub. Once you open an account, you gain access to this and other investment tools. However, if you want to do it yourself the old-fashioned way, you can do that too. You would start your search online by googling mutual fund companies. There are more than sixteen thousand mutual funds in the investing universe, and not all are created equal. How do you narrow that down to a manageable number? Start with the most-experienced and best-known mutual fund companies. There are many great ones out there, but I will give you a short list of the largest, most popular, oldest, and generally lowest-cost fund families in the United States (*Disclaimer:* This is not an endorsement or recommendation of any mutual fund company or product; it's simply a basic and incomplete list of well-established fund families in the United States to get you started):

- American Funds
- PIMCO
- Delaware
- Putnam
- Fidelity Investments
- T. Rowe Price
- Franklin
- Templeton
- Vanguard
- MFS Investments.

These fund families each have several mutual funds to choose from. They have stock mutual funds, bond mutual funds, sector funds, index funds, asset allocation funds, balanced funds, money market funds, and target-date funds. That may sound like a lot, but take it as good news that you can find a fund that is the right fit for you. Each investor is unique and will have a particular need to help complete his or her portfolio. Let me break down what each of these broad categories of funds means:

- Stock mutual fund
  A mutual fund made up of only stocks and cash.

- Bond mutual fund
  A mutual fund made up of only bonds and cash.

- Balanced fund
  A mutual fund made up of stocks, bonds, and cash.

- Money market fund
  Cash equivalent funds meant to keep volatility low with each share price set to $1. Used mainly for capital preservation and diversification.

- Sector fund
  Fund assets are derived from a particular sector of the market, for example, health care, real estate, utilities, or precious metals.

- Index fund
  A fund in which the holdings of the fund match a particular index or benchmark, for example, the S&P 500 stock market index or the Dow Jones Industrial Average.

- Asset allocation fund
  A fund with stocks, bonds, and cash that is balanced in such a way as to achieve a desired risk tolerance objective such as aggressive, moderate, or conservative. Aggressive allocation funds will have greater weight in stocks, whereas more-conservative allocation funds will have greater weight in cash and bonds. This type of fund is self-rebalancing to meet the stated risk tolerance. *Self-rebalancing* means that the manager of the fund will go in periodically to buy and sell stocks or bonds to correct the market effects on the underlying assets. As we have discussed, stocks change value much more frequently than do bonds and cash assets, so they tend to appreciate or depreciate much faster within the fund. That causes an imbalance in the original allocation and can misalign the fund to the objective if left unchecked for too long.

- Target-date fund
  This is a fund that is allocated with stocks, bonds, and cash to achieve a reasonable rate of return with a specified time horizon in mind. A target-date fund that is pegged to the year 2045 will have a greater weighting in stocks than a fund pegged to the year 2025. The longer the time horizon, the more aggressive the fund will start out, but as time goes by, the fund will become rebalanced to be more conservative as the anticipated withdrawal date approaches. This type of fund is self-adjusting to meet the stated time horizon.

In order to do an effective screening of available mutual funds, you need to narrow down your search according to your objectives, your time horizon, and the type of fund that you might be looking for. You can find all you need to know about a fund (and then some) in its **prospectus**. All mutual funds are required to come with a prospectus by law. In fact, you are supposed to receive the mutual fund prospectus and review it carefully *before* investing. The prospectus tells you about the major holdings of the fund, gives you the manager's biography, mentions the objective and the style of the fund, and discusses any fees, any restrictions, or any other material information that can help you make an informed decision about the investment prospects of the fund. The prospectus will also cover what risks the fund may have. Always understand your risk. Different funds have different risks. Just because you invest in a mutual fund doesn't mean there are no risks. You can garner a good deal of information from just the first few pages of the fund prospectus.

Let's see what kind of information we can discern by looking at a fund objective statement. For example, a mutual fund's prospectus might say something like this:

"The fund seeks to achieve growth and income through the investment in established companies that are uniquely positioned within their industries to continue to capture market share and expand."

What does this objective and style statement tell you about the underlying assets in this particular fund? There are a couple of hints there to give you an indication of the type of investments that would probably be held in this fund. Take a few minutes to answer the following questions and see if you can sort it out on your own:

- What is the fund objective?
- What is the fund's investment style?
- What types of assets would most likely be held in this fund?
- What type of investor might prefer to invest in this fund?
- What type of time horizon might the investor need in order to realize a reasonable rate of return with this fund?

Yes, all those questions can be answered by reading that short objective statement in the front of the prospectus. Ask yourself why you think the statement leads you to believe certain things about the fund.

The first clue about the fund's objective is in the first few words: "the fund seeks to achieve growth and income." That is the fund's objective. That was an easy one, and I'm sure you got it right away. But how about the style? What types of assets would be in this fund?

The fund's style is hinted at in the phrase *established companies*. Established companies are older, larger, and generally well-known. The statement doesn't mention anything about global or offshore companies, so you can assume the fund invests in domestic large-cap stocks. One thing to note is that the style needs to match the objective, so we're not looking only for large companies that would grow; we're also looking for companies that would pay income. How do companies pay income on their stocks? They pay income to shareholders of stock through dividends. Dividends are payouts of company profits

111

to shareholders. Rather than reinvesting all the profits of the company in order to finance expansion, many large established companies will also pay dividends. Dividends provide income to stockholders.

So, we've figured out the objective and the style of the fund, as well as the types of assets that might be held by the fund. How about the type of investor who might prefer this type of a fund? Well, the investor likely has a long time horizon to invest or has a greater risk tolerance. Because this fund is invested in stocks, although established large company stocks, there will still be some volatility in the share price as it experiences the market. Market conditions, including those that are industry specific, and overall economic conditions cannot be avoided in a large-cap growth and income fund. This investor should have a few years to leave the money there and a healthy understanding of the risks of ownership.

Mutual funds in general should be held a minimum of three to five years to produce an effective and reasonable rate of return. Sometimes that length of time needs to be extended because of unexpected market downturns. Any mutual fund investor, save those in money market mutual funds, should have flexibility in his or her time horizon should the market make unexpected turns. There are two things that you can trust to be absolutely true about the market: it goes up and it goes down. If you can figure out with any accuracy when it will do either, you will be the wealthiest person in the world. This feat has yet to be achieved with any long-term consistency. Your goal is to achieve consistent returns over the long term. That means gains you achieve in up markets will offset losses in down markets. "Buy and hold" must be your strategy if you intend to use mutual funds in your portfolio; they are long-term commitments. Mutual funds can be great options for long-term goals, but don't try trading in and out of them a lot or you're bound to end up frustrated!

Almost Everything You Ever Wanted to Know about Investing in Real Estate

Real estate investing is such a funny subject. Many people feel that real estate investment is a sure thing. There is an old saying, "Buy land because God isn't making any more of it." There could be some wisdom to that directive, but depending on your understanding of real estate, the tax implications, the use of the land or property, the intended holding period, and the availability of financing, you may find yourself in over your head. If you forget everything else in this section, remember this one thing: *real estate is not a sure thing.* It's an investment just like any other, with a lot to consider before jumping in. It is also typically more expensive and risky than your average asset, with more upkeep required than a simple stock, bond, or mutual fund.

Buying a home with a white picket fence and a two-car garage used to be the American dream. This was a common perception back in the 1950s, when the government was a little less involved, money was a little harder to come by (and therefore more valuable), and prices weren't astronomical for the average American. Back in 1950, families could thrive on one salary, buy a house and a car, and still have plenty of wiggle room if the economy took a little downturn. A quote from reference. com[3] states:

> "The average annual salary in the United States in 1950 was \$3,210. The average cost of a gallon of gas in 1950 was 18 cents, while the cost of a new car was \$1,510 and a house would cost roughly \$8,450."

That was seventy years ago. According to the Census's American Community Survey[4], the median household income for the United States was \$62,843 in 2019—the latest data available as of this writing. According to statista.com[5], the average price of a house in 2019 was \$383,900. Comparing the figures from 1950 to those from 2019, you can see the income disparity and how housing prices have grown at a rate much greater than has income for the individuals buying the homes. In 1950, the average home price was 2.63 times the average household income. In 2019, it was 6.11 times that amount. What does this mean? It means fewer people can afford to buy homes in the United States these days, and it's been progressively getting worse. What could that mean for longer-term housing prices? It means something has got to give. As I illustrated in a previous example, if you have a lot of houses on the market for sale but not a lot of eligible buyers, you have a buyer's market and the prices will eventually come down. Something else could happen in a sustained situation like that. We've experienced this "something else" for the past fifteen years or so. I'll bet you have

---

[3] What was the Average Annual Salary in the U.S. in 1950? www.reference.com/business-finance/average-annual-salary-u-s-1950-76b0654d84ee2912

[4] https://www.census.gov/acs/www/data/data-tables-and-tools/narrative-profiles/ "American Community Survey, Household Income in the United States in 2015-2019

[5] https://www.statista.com/statistics/240991/average-sales-prices-of-new-homes-sold-in-the-us/"Average sales price of new homes sold in US from 1965 to 2021"

a guess as to what it might be. It is something that happened on a grotesque scale—one previously unseen by the markets—back in 2004–7.

If you guessed that government regulations, and as a result, banks, might loosen up the requirements for larger-than-usual or longer-than-usual loans to make it possible for people with less income to afford to live in these higher-priced homes, then you'd be right. There would also be companies capitalizing on the loosened regulations by inventing new financing vehicles and customized loans, such as "stated income loans" or "interest-only mortgages." Some might call this creative financing. I call it fudging the numbers. Either way, the effects, as witnessed by the Great Recession, can be devastating. The numbers don't lie. I have said this before, I know, but you have to run the numbers before you make *any* investment, and that includes your house.

There are a great many ways to invest in real estate, and each has its particular set of considerations. Let's take the most common real estate investments one at a time. Following is a list of them:

- land ownership
- home ownership
- rental property (residential or commercial)
- flipping houses
- business ownership
- holding a note
- owning shares in REITs.

At first glance, investing in land seems the most simple and straightforward investment option. In many ways it can be. You own a piece of land, you pay the property taxes on it, you sell it, you collect the profit. That makes sense. Pretty simple. Owning land can also present many other possibilities that touch on the other types of real estate investing. For instance, you could own land that is large enough to support a farm but have no interest in owning or running a farm. You can rent out your land to a farmer, and he or she can farm the land and pay you for its use. The same goes for lumber or any type of commercial or residential endeavor. You could rent your land to people who want to put a camper on it and live there. You could rent or lease the land to a developer who wants to build commercial space. There are a great many possibilities when you own land other than simply selling it. Of course, you always have that option too.

But there are downsides to consider. What happens if you own land and later on it is found to contain some sort of hazard? You have to deal with the municipality and the state regulators to find out how to remedy the hazard or remove it. You also run the risk of not being able to sell or rent the land if it has a history of being hazardous. There is also the matter of squatters. Squatter's rights vary from state to state. If you own land, or any other real estate for that matter, you should check it regularly to be aware of anyone using it without your knowledge. This could be a sticky situation that can sometimes lead to the loss of your property. See, even something as simple as owning land has its risks.

Residential real estate investing is still seen as a major accomplishment in today's society. It can be an exhilarating experience every time, whether it's your first or fifteenth house. When you buy a home in which you intend to live, it's a harbinger of new adventure, a new life, a new beginning. Long-term historical returns on home purchases average around 6 percent in the United States after expenses. The big problem is the way the average American views a home purchase.

Some people view a home as a living expense, while others view it as an investment asset. Both perspectives are somewhat correct in that you have to live somewhere, but either way there has to be an accurate assessment of ROI, or return on investment. And this is where problems can arise. Many people calculate ROI simply as the following:

Price sold – Price paid = Profit or ROI

If only it were that simple! With a house purchase, you must take into consideration all the costs associated with home ownership. Not only the cost of maintenance and upgrades to the property, but also the cost of taxes, insurance, and any necessary association fees. These costs add up to significant amounts of money and must be included in the total if you are to get an accurate assessment of ROI on the property. Don't forget the amount you pay in interest if you carry a mortgage. Many times, people end up paying half or two-thirds of the purchase price in interest to the mortgage holder. The new formula for ROI then becomes as follows:

Price sold – (Price paid + All expenses during ownership) = ROI

This is why I refer to any real estate purchase as a maintenance asset. You can't just purchase a property and leave it there without supervision or maintenance. It would fall into disarray. That includes land. For some people, real estate is their preferred investment vehicle. It can be very lucrative for the right investor who is willing to handle all the maintenance and governmental requirements for real estate ownership, rental, leasing, sale, and even usage. Additionally, it is a tangible asset. You can see it, you can live in it or on it, and you can touch it, feel it, and physically draw benefit from it daily. That is certainly worth something.

In addition to all the upkeep of a property, you must be mindful of the market in which your asset resides, both local and national. Many factors can affect the value of your property. Some of these include the quality of local schools, crime rates, federal government policies and local city ordinances, property taxes, demographics, and neighbors. Something as simple as your neighbors painting their house shocking lime green could affect the value of your house. Typically, a house is the largest single asset a person owns. That's a whole lot of concentrated money in one pot with no real return until it's sold. I know you're thinking, *but what if I rent it out to someone? That's real return before the sale.* Yes, that may be true, and it's a great segway to our discussion on residential rental property.

This type of real estate investing can be very attractive, especially for investors who are looking for an income stream from their assets. But like everything else, it has its challenges. Let's talk about what to look out for.

In addition to all the considerations you will have to keep in mind when owning a property, if you become a residential landlord, you will also need to stay on top of the laws in your state governing landlord's and renter's rights. If a renter becomes delinquent, which can happen even in the best of economic times, you must know your rights and your tenant's rights, as well as the procedure and time line for eviction. If things go even farther south and you find yourself dealing with a difficult tenant, you may be concerned that your home is being destroyed beyond reasonable repair. In some cases, you may need to hire a lawyer to recoup losses. Residential tenants can be a sticky business.

Of course, if you do your due diligence and carefully conduct background checks, call references, and screen for the best tenants, you can also end up with an amazing renter who may provide you a steady, reliable stream of income for years. People generally don't like change, and they certainly don't like to move if they don't have to, so good tenants can be sticky too—and that's good business.

Although we've touched on many of the pitfalls and perks, this list is not exhaustive. And my personal experience is not the same as every real estate investor's. I will share this tidbit, however, that took me quite by surprise. Some towns or municipalities may assign utility expenses to the property where the utility service was delivered, as opposed to assigning them to the person who used the service. Check with your town or municipality to see how it applies unpaid bills, fines, or charges for utility misuse, because if they charge it to the property, you may not know that you have an unpaid lien. When you go to sell the property, you have to satisfy those liens before the title can be transferred. Meanwhile, your tenant is long gone and may have already received his or her security deposit back, leaving you stuck with paying the bill. A good rule of thumb when taking on renters is to have a contingency plan and an emergency budget in place. You may do this by putting aside a portion of the rental income you receive each month for a time when the unexpected inevitably arises.

If you are simply in the rental business to make money and aren't too concerned about the pristine condition of your property or sensitive about taking money from a government housing fund, you may want to participate in a program like Section 8. This type of housing involves a rental agreement between you and the government in return for providing your rental property to lower-income tenants. The government subsidizes the tenant's rent, and you receive a fair market value rental income (typically with an adjustment for cost of living) deposited directly into your account like clockwork every month. The government backs the contract and sees to it that standard rules and regulations are followed by your tenants. These programs vary from state to state and are called different things, but they can be very lucrative. The main problem with these types of rental agreements is the fact of constantly changing laws governing public housing and allowances. You may have different standards of management varying from city to city or state to state. Not all government programs are run efficiently or correctly, so that's a risk.

Commercial real estate ownership and leasing is a whole different animal. Since you are either selling or renting your property to businesses, the government is a lot more lenient with regard to how you protect your asset. Compared to residential renters who have government protections to prevent them from being kicked out onto the street (essentially being made homeless) if they fail to pay rent, businesses that rent property from you have no such protection. If they become delinquent, you can change the locks and keep them out. It takes a whole lot of procedure and jumping through hoops in similar situations with residential tenants.

Here are some things to keep in mind if you want to invest in commercial property, especially if you plan to rent it out: *everything* is more expensive when deemed "commercial." That can be good and bad for a commercial landlord. It can be good because rents will be higher. But guess what? The insurance for the property is also going to be higher. So too will be the utilities, municipal services, and taxes and all the other maintenance expenses. From the very first transaction— the property purchase—you can expect costs associated with ownership to be twice the total cost of a similar transaction in the residential market. Be ready to work these increased costs into your investment and ROI numbers. Remember, whether you're renting out residential or commercial real estate, your true return on investment (ROI) is calculated as follows:

$$\frac{\text{Annual rental income} - \text{Annual property expenses}}{\text{Price paid}} = \text{Annual ROI}$$

Let me give you a simple example with a residential property: You purchase a quaint three-bedroom house in an average middle-class neighborhood for $150,000 cash (just to keep it really simple, however uncommon this may be). Your fair market rental income would be $1,200 per month or $14,400 per year. It costs you $200 per month in maintenance, utilities, and municipal service. Taxes are also $200 per month. Your annual ROI then looks like this:

$$\frac{\$14,400 - (\$400 \times 12)}{\$150,000} = \frac{\$14,400 - \$4,800}{\$150,000} = 6.4\% \text{ AAR}$$

Not a bad return in today's interest rate environment. Now, you also need to keep in mind that your ROI goes down with every month that you didn't collect rent or your property sat vacant. It may take you a month or two to find a tenant or to renovate a room. And don't forget about the reserve account you need for unexpected expenses that pop up. Expenses you should be prepared for include everything from minor repairs and appliance replacement to a new roof and legal assistance if necessary. These reserves can cut into your ROI as well, but if you are able to sell the property without significantly tapping into the reserves, you can add them back to your total ROI for the life of the property.

With commercial property, the calculation is very similar; however, a great many more complications and expenses are involved. Let me give you a commercial real estate example: You buy a small street-front strip mall with four identical retail units available to rent for $250,000. To lure in tenants quickly, it's common for commercial building owners to offer incentives like "build to suit" or "no rent during build-out." Those incentives are direct expenses for you, but you're willing to put a little money into securing tenants as quickly as possible. Your gamble works to your benefit and you get a hair salon, a boutique clothier, a jewelry store, and a small cafe to sign rental agreements. The cafe owners will take the longest to build out their space since they will have to install a grease trap to be compliant with local regulations for food service establishments. Additionally, before you can allow your tenants to open their businesses, they each have to furnish liability insurance that covers them and you in the case of damage, as well as occupational certificates from the local municipality. It takes four months for all your tenants to open for business. You're charging each of them the same $2,500 monthly rent (to keep it simple). Your ROI formula then looks like this:

$$\frac{\$30,000 - (\$2,500 \times 4)}{\$250,000} = \frac{\$30,000 - \$10,000}{\$250,000} = \frac{\$20,000}{\$250,000} = 8\% \text{ AAR}$$

Eight percent is a great rate of return. However, this is a very simplistic example and in no way touches on accounting for every little complication that could pop up and eat away at your ROI. Remember, I said that *everything* in business is more expensive! That means your reserves have to be larger because more expensive assets cost more to maintain.

Rehabbing fixer-uppers and flipping properties is yet another way to invest in real estate. Of course, this typically involves much more upfront investment and personal effort to be successful, but for the right investor, it can be quite lucrative. Hey, I'm as much a fan of Chip and Jojo as anyone else is, but they put in a lot of work and they don't show you all the unforeseen problems they run into tearing down and fixing up undesirable houses, let alone the issues they must encounter with all the contractors, homeowners, and government agencies putting in their own two cents along the way. No, they don't air any of the bad investments that they've had to eat. They've been at it for a while; no one wins on every investment.

If buying fixer-uppers is something you might be interested in, be sure to give yourself plenty of wiggle room on the first one. You'll be paying for a learning curve and also for some inevitable rookie mistakes once you take the plunge, so don't anticipate wild returns right out of the gate. Temper your expectations. You'll get better at it the more you do it.

I have limited experience in this arena, but I can give you a few pointers, as follows, to help you get off on the right foot:

1. Location is key. The state of the house isn't quite as important as the desirability of the neighborhood (barring structural damage).

2. Always get an inspection before purchase. You want to know what you're walking into so you can accurately estimate renovation expenses.
3. Do as much of the simple work as you can yourself. Demo, cleanup, painting, yard work, simple landscaping—all these easy-to-handle things can help you save money for the real projects that give you larger returns on your investment.
4. Pay the experts for expert work. For those projects that are out of your comfort zone, be sure to shop around and get reliable contractors who'll do a great job, whether it be for a new roof, a new kitchen, a bathroom renovation, or plumbing or electrical work. Don't go halfway on the key things that make a house more attractive to buyers.
5. Make sure you understand the property's zoning and conservation restrictions. Nothing can derail a rehab project like finding out about restrictions after the renovations have been done. Historical properties and those that touch conservation land can be the trickiest. Be sure to get informed about your rights and obligations before purchase.

Keep it simple. Don't overimprove a property as compared to other properties in the neighborhood. You won't get any additional return if you invest more than is expected for certain features. Comfortable kitchens and bathrooms are key to maximizing returns on investment properties. Other improvements can help, but the ROI on other individual projects aren't as high as they are for kitchens and baths. And while we're still on the subject of ROI, let's talk a bit about the different ways that you can finance your real estate purchase and who will be involved (and will rightly need to be paid) to help you along the way.

In the simplest of transactions, you can buy and sell property for cash with the other interested party. This would be the easiest and quickest way to get yourself into the real estate world. Someone has a property you are interested in; they want to sell it; you both sit down and negotiate the price and the terms; you hand over the cash; they sign over the deed; and you're done! Congratulations! You own some real estate! Ah, if only it were always so simple.

In this example, there are only two people involved in the transaction: the buyer and the seller. These two people are going to be involved in every real estate purchase transaction. Oftentimes, this is the way properties are sold when they are put on auction by the government because of unpaid liens, back taxes, or other types of foreclosure. This isn't the most common way to purchase property, but it is a possible avenue to acquiring real estate.

But how does the average person get into real estate? How does one know where to start? How does a person get the money to buy the property if he or she doesn't have enough in cash? How does a person find his or her ideal property? How does he or she navigate the governmental requirements for purchasing property? How does he or she make the transaction legal and official?

All these questions have very specific answers. If the buyer is qualified, he or she will be able to buy a property with the help of a team of people. Similarly, there will be questions on the seller's side too. How does he or she ensure that the deal is done and that he or she has no more legal obligation to the property? How can he or she find qualified buyers? How does he or she let the government know that he or she is no longer responsible for the taxes on the property? How does he or she advertise his or her desire to sell the property?

People often falsely believe that they can easily buy and sell property and that it doesn't require any special skills or knowledge. I assure you that navigating the complex real estate market takes time, effort, patience, and know-how. So, if you plan to go it alone, plan to encounter a steep learning curve. Very rarely do properties sell quickly without the proper attention, an announcement, or a listing on the national market register for properties for sale.

Most people do not have the massive amounts of cash needed to buy a property outright just lying around. They first need money or someone to loan them money in order to become qualified buyers. A qualified buyer is someone who has been given preliminary approval for a mortgage within a certain range. A **mortgage broker** will be the first person you consult if you want to assess your ability to invest in real estate. A mortgage broker is someone who either works for a bank or works independently representing several banks to connect potential buyers with potential lenders. If you need to borrow money to buy a property, you need someone to lend it to you. A mortgage broker will help you find a lender if your credit is worthy. Remember that we talked earlier at length about how important your credit is. Qualifying for a mortgage is a very, very good reason to protect it!

Once you've been prequalified for a mortgage and know your available range of credit, you can begin your property search. These days, with the help of the internet, you can do this on your own, but I would advise that you work with a realtor. A **realtor** can be invaluable in helping you navigate all your options, in answering the questions you must ask to avoid purchasing a money pit, and in locating your ideal property. Realtors have instant access to the open real estate market, and they can whittle down your search once you've explained what you are looking for and what you're qualified to buy. The seller is likely going to have a realtor on his or her side helping him or her navigate the seller's market and lead a qualified buyer like you to his or her door. You should have similar representation advocating for your wants and needs. You will have what is called a **buyer's agent**, and the seller will have a **seller's agent**.

Of course, realtors, or real estate agents, don't work for free. You should know that a portion of the proceeds from the sale of the property will be paid to the realtor. Typically, these fees are paid only by the seller, but as with anything in a real estate deal, this is negotiable. For residential property, the total agent fees are usually around 6 percent, and for commercial property, the total agent fees are around 10 percent. If there is one agent representing both sides, he or she gets the full percentage unless it has been negotiated down. If there are two agents, they usually split the total percentage. When you're talking about hundreds of thousands of dollars, that commission can be quite a lot, so when you hire a realtor, make sure that his or her services and fees are clearly laid out. You will also want to outline expectations, terms of the contract, and stipulations to terminate the contract or to rescind the fee if the realtor fails to perform according to the contract. This might seem very involved, but it is important to protect yourself and understand exactly what realtors can and cannot do for you.

Most of the time a realtor's contract will be good for six months, at which time it may be terminated or renewed upon review. Usually the realtor won't get paid a dime if the house doesn't sell or if he or she doesn't find you the property you want. This structure is an incentive for the realtor to find what you need. If the six-month contract expires and you feel you need to change agents or take the property off the market, then that is the price the agent pays. I think it's quite a risk they're taking, literally betting their income on their performance. But that is the way it works. You should be perfectly clear about expectations, how and when the agent gets paid, as well as the amount before you sign a sales agreement with a realtor. Alternatively, if the realtor turns out to be a deadbeat and doesn't do anything with your property and it sits vacant and unsold for six months, that costs you money, especially if you have a mortgage. You have to be very selective and comfortable with the person you hire to represent you. You must trust that this individual will get the job done in whatever market environment exists.

Once your agent has found your perfect property, you make an offer to the seller based on your prequalified mortgage range.

Your agent should only show you properties within your approved range. If you make an offer on a property and it is accepted, that is the first step in a long process until closing. From experience, I can say that until it's closed, it ain't sold, so don't count your chickens until the fat lady sings. You also should understand that although realtors are very knowledgeable and can typically navigate the subtle nuances of a real estate purchase with ease, they are not lawyers. You will want to consult with a **real estate lawyer** to make sure your contract is sound and that you have been protected against fraud, unreasonable terms, or buying a lemon. This is important and well worth the cost. For my last home purchase, it cost me $950 for the lawyer, and he walked through all the contracts with the seller's lawyer throughout the process and accompanied me at the closing. You don't want to buy a house that has an unreported history of mold or chemical seepage that you only discover years later when you are terribly sick and unsure how you got that way. You'll have no recourse if there isn't some type of protection built into your purchase agreement.

Additionally, you will hire an **inspector** prior to the purchase to assess the structure and roof, the condition of the home, and the inhabitability of the property. An inspection is an absolute must if you plan to buy a turnkey house, especially with a mortgage. The lender will require an inspection and a termination clause in the contract in case anything is found to be unsound or suspect about the property and you still want to move forward with the purchase. Keep in mind that inspectors are not all created equal. If the condo tragedy in Surfside, Florida, in the summer of 2021 taught us anything, it's that finding a reputable and honorable inspector is an absolute must.

Now, you've dotted all your *i*'s and crossed all your *t*'s and you're ready for closing. You will go to a **title office** to sign all the final documents and collect your keys. The title office is the company that will file all your legal paperwork with the government to record the sale and change ownership of the property. It also provides title insurance (to be sure that the title or deed of the property is not subject to any liens or any other party claiming ownership to the property). The title office is also in charge of holding your deposit and mortgage in escrow (an account held by a third party to await disbursement of funds after certain conditions are met) for the seller and checking over all the required paperwork to be sure it's in good order. You guessed it, the title office doesn't do all this for free: they get a fee from the proceeds of the sale as well. This fee is part of what is referred to as the "closing costs." Closing costs include agent's fees, title fees, lawyer's fees, bank fees, document filing fees, government surcharges and taxes, and insurance requirements.

Once you've signed the mountain of papers that your lawyer hopefully reviewed and translated for you, you get the keys and the property is yours. That's quite a process. It can be time-consuming and, at times, intimidating. Be careful and be aware if you plan to go any part of it alone. There's always some unknown waiting around the corner, so it helps to have a qualified team to guide you toward the right decisions for you and your family. No one wants to get stuck with someone else's headache, let alone pay huge sums of money for it!

I want to shift gears here and flip the scenario. I have spoken a lot about typical types of real estate investing, but there are other ways to make money in real estate that can be lucrative but are less common. What if you had the means to help qualified people achieve their dreams of buying a home? What if you were to play the part of the bank? What if you could hold the note on a property and collect interest for an extended period of time? You could likely turn it into a pretty reliable stream of income if you had the right screening process and qualification system.

There are plenty of worthy people with steady incomes who would like to purchase property but lack the sum of money or the comfort level with banks or mortgage brokers for whatever reason. I'm not talking about people who destroyed their credit;

I mean hardworking everyday people who have been caught in a bad situation through no fault of their own.

The government has gone from one extreme to the other. In 2006, deregulation of the lending business had reached such a fever pitch that banks were lending out more than seventy-two times the amount that they had in their reserves. They were severely out of their depth and unable, therefore, to back those mortgages in the case of default. In its frenzy, the industry continued to chant long-held beliefs that mortgages were the safest loans available with almost zero risk. That was true when regulations required people applying for mortgages to actually prove they had income and were creditworthy. But by 2006, all reasonability seemed to have flown out the window. I personally witnessed clients of mine who were making $35,000 gross annual salaries and were being approved for second and third home purchases of $300,000. Just looking at those numbers makes me dizzy.

So, what did the government do after the housing and financial markets finally blew up in 2008–9? They pulled a 180 and basically said, "No one is getting a mortgage." You nearly had to be Warren Buffett on paper to get minimal approval. This opened up an opportunity for investors who had some means to offer reasonable term mortgages to perfectly creditworthy people in the market for a primary residence or a first-time home. When you decide to become the lender instead of the buyer, you are said to "hold the note" on a property. Essentially you are holding onto the promissory note that legally states that the borrower (home buyer) will pay you back, when, with what frequency, and at what interest rate. The promissory note legally binds the purchaser to the terms of the agreement. In case of buyer breach of this agreement, the property is subject to foreclosure and ownership defaults to the lender. It's exactly what the banks do. You can be the bank, and depending on the terms, you can make a nice, steady stream of income that in my view has relatively low risk (people don't like to be kicked out of their homes, so they tend to pay)—and at a greater rate of interest than many other investments of similar risk levels today. It takes due diligence, proper screening, and excellent legal counsel, but it can be a worthwhile investment.

You can also hold the note through **owner financing** of a property that you already own but want to sell directly without the involvement of a bank. This works best if you own a property outright (you have no mortgage obligation) and would like to sell it while also creating a stream of income for yourself, instead of receiving a large lump sum that you'd have to otherwise invest. This option becomes increasingly attractive as one gets older because owner financing of a property to a worthy buyer can be spread out over a common mortgage term and can provide income from a pretty illiquid investment. What I mean by this is that a house is not something that one can sell at any given time on any given day in any given marketplace. A house is not quickly turned into cash in most instances. It can, however, help to finance someone's retirement. So, we find that the average American has a lot of his or her net worth tied up in one or two properties without much other savings. If someone is lucky enough to hold a second property, then he or she can opt to owner-finance the property to a well-qualified and thoroughly vetted buyer. Then the seller will receive what is the equivalent of an annuity, or a steady stream of payments with a stated interest rate for a set number of years. Let's work through an example, including some of the risks involved, to make it clearer:

Charlie is a seventy-year-old snowbird who splits his time between Ohio and Florida. He and his partner Melinda traveled back and forth for about three years before deciding this year to brave the steamy summer and stay south the full year. Surprisingly, Charlie loves it since his health seems to fair better in Florida. So, to make things easier and more affordable for everyone, Charlie rented the Ohio home to his son, Stanford. Now that Stanford and his family are settled in there, Stanford has expressed interest in buying the property from his father.

Charlie told Stanford that he'd consider the idea. After he talked it over with Melinda and chatted with others, the couple heard about a friend with a similar situation. The friend sold her northern home directly to her daughter and now receives a nice check for two thousand dollars every month that helps her retire well. Charlie never considered owner-financing the house to Stanford mostly because he didn't know the option existed, but he knows that Stanford earns a good living and is very prudent with his money. Charlie certainly could use the extra income! After talking it over, father and son agree on a twenty-year mortgage at 5 percent interest. Stanford is ecstatic that he doesn't have to deal with the red tape at the bank, and his dad is overjoyed to have the boost in income for the next twenty years!

Of course, this is a simple example. And normally I advise caution when getting into any type of business arrangement with family. But for certain situations and individuals, it can be a great solution as well as an investment. Charlie would still want to double-check Stanford's creditworthiness, credit history, and credit report. This is important for transparency and also to protect both Stanford and Charlie, especially if Stanford has siblings!

One risk that Charlie will have to consider is prepayment risk. If Stanford accelerates his payments and wants to pay the mortgage off early or sell the property, then Charlie should be prepared to make other arrangements to compensate for the loss in income. Very few people who are not in financial services can effectively stretch a lump sum of money out over a lifetime. If prepayment should happen, Charlie should consult with a financial professional to discuss and plan how to replace the lost monthly income with the lump sum for the remainder of the twenty years. Charlie also has to consider the risk of default associated with any type of loan. He should have it written in the purchase agreement that in the event of default, ownership reverts to the lender, just as it would if it were a bank holding the mortgage note. Yes, if Stanford were to default on the loan (not pay it back), then Charlie would foreclose on the property and retain ownership once again.

Owner financing is sometimes the only option if a property is uninsurable for some reason and cash buyers are scarce. There are situations in which a specific type of property may be attractive and salable but cannot be insured and therefore doesn't qualify for a traditional mortgage. That leaves cash purchase as the only buying option, unless the owner is willing to finance the sale. For instance, in my coastal Florida town, some waterfront property is uninsurable if it has a modular or manufactured home on it. The homes are perfectly adorable and habitable, but the risk of flood or destruction in a hurricane makes the residence too big of a risk for insurance companies. So, what happens to the homeowners in these situations? They are forced to be self-insured or to tear down their modular or manufactured homes and build something new according to current code standards. That requires a whole lot of money. Many homeowners opt to self-insure and take their chances. If a hurricane does blow the house away, they still own the land after all—and the land is what has the higher value of the property. These homeowners either had to purchase these homes outright or finance them directly from the sellers.

So now that you've read all of this but you're not too keen on all the heavy lifting, there is good news, namely that if you want to get into the wonderful world of real estate and reap the benefits of the market, you can be a real estate investor without personally owning any property. You can invest your money in a sector fund that is restricted to investing in real estate holdings, real property, property management companies, and other companies directly involved in the real estate market. These mutual fund–type investments are called **real estate investment trusts**, or **REITs**. REITs allow an investor to put money in but not concern himself with the day-to-day management, maintenance, or repair of real property. All the benefits and none of the work? Sign me up! Actually, a REIT is a great way to have exposure to the real estate market but shield yourself from the pains of human emotional involvement, physical maintenance, and too much government interference. REITs are also a great way to diversify a portfolio that may be overly concentrated in blue-chip stocks or in the S&P 500. Of course, keep in mind that REITs can be illiquid and are also subject to risk.

I'm so glad we had the opportunity to talk at length about real estate in this chapter. Buying or selling real estate is such a big and important event in the lives of most people. It can be a complex marketplace. But keep in mind that this discussion is in no way all-encompassing. There are many creative ways to benefit from the world of real estate. I want to reiterate that real estate, in almost all its forms, requires some degree of maintenance, oversight, and continued investment to realize a sound profit. Now that you have the intel, you will be able to choose the best path for yourself.

Uncommon and Other Types of Investments

Now that we've been through the ins and outs of some of the more typical investment types, in this chapter we are going to talk about some of the less common, more complicated, and oddball things you hear about in the world of investments. In this section we will focus on one of the biggest investments that regular folks like you and me will ever make in their lives: owning and running a business.

Entrepreneurship

The dream of one day opening a business of his very own, of making it big and calling the shots, has captured the imagination of many an average Joe. *Entrepreneur* is the fancy term given to the brave souls who venture out on their own to pitch products, services, and ideas of their own design to the masses. However, owning a business and running a business are two very different things. One is sexy and glamorous, whereas the other can be anything but. Imagine yourself working a hundred-hour week, wrangling employees, pushing sales, training new hires, and maintaining superior quality at reasonable costs, all while keeping a smile on your face and waking up with the motivation to do it all again tomorrow (and day in and day out until the damn thing works).

Opening your own business is the one investment that has both the highest possible risks and the highest possible rewards. You know what they say: if it were easy, everybody'd be doing it. With start-up businesses, the odds are unfortunately stacked against you. When I talk about the risks and rewards of starting your own business, I'm not just talking about monetary risks and rewards. Business ownership can get very precarious. Entrepreneurship is a wild ride. It can either break families and ruin relationships or bring families and friends closer together. To start and run a business, you must be careful but a risk-taker, prudent but decisive, and optimistic yet cautious. You must be all things and none of them rigidly. What I mean is that once you are in business, it's business. You have to treat the health of your business as if it were the health of your child. You must be willing to make difficult and unpopular decisions. You must be willing and able to have uncomfortable conversations and question everything. You must trust but also be aware. Sometimes, depending on the type of business, you must grapple for every last dime of revenue, all the while maintaining a great brand and public image. It is like walking a tightrope when the rope is on fire and there's a lion tamer behind you cracking his whip. It can be exhilarating! It can also be terrifying and the most rewarding achievement you will ever experience. It could be totally worth it or totally worthless. Do you see what I'm getting at? Business ownership can have the most risk and the most reward.

Going into business for yourself can be a powerful, courageous, and completely insane prospect, and not in that order. The odds are seemingly insurmountable, yet people continue to do it and succeed. Why is that? According to a 2011

Huffington Post article titled "Five Big Myths About American Small Businesses[6],"

> "Large businesses only employ about 38 percent of the private sector workforce[,] while small businesses employ 53 percent of the workforce. In fact, over 99 percent of employing organizations are small businesses and more than 95 percent of these businesses have fewer than 10 employees. The reality is that most Americans are employed by a very small business that has little in common with the tiny sliver of the business demographic represented by corporate America."

People just don't want to work for corporate America. Or is it the American spirit that fuels our economy? Whatever it is, people are starting their own businesses, and some of these are actually working!

If and when you decide to go into business for yourself, you'll have many factors to consider. One thing I learned from owning and running businesses is that it seems that small businesses are in business to keep other businesses (and the government!) in business. You will want to consider your business structure and its effect on your personal income taxes and your corporate income taxes. Yes, of course, you have to pay taxes even when you're in business for yourself! You know what they say, there are only two certainties in life: death and taxes. There's no way around it unless you're Donald Trump (too soon?).

I should mention here that our current laws and tax system do favor corporations over individuals. When you work for yourself, you are able to use much of your income for business expenses and only pay taxes on what is truly leftover income, or net profit. I am not an accountant (I did get an A in that one

---

[6] Arslan, Kristie. "Five Big Myths About American Small Businesses", *Huffington Post,* May 24, 2011.

accounting class though), so I highly suggest that you consult one before you establish your corporation. There are pros and cons to opening a sole proprietor business, a C corporation, an S corporation, an LLC (limited liability corporation), or a partnership. Small business is the engine that keeps the United States' economy growing, so if you have the entrepreneurial spirit, look into going into business for yourself. To be successful, you'll just have to show up earlier than everyone else, leave later than everyone else, practice, fail, practice some more, fail some more, learn, grow, prioritize, and endure. Then you'll be successful. Also, keep this in mind: success is relative. There is success even in failure, as long as you are learning and growing.

Hobbies and Collectibles (Are They Really Investments?)

With all the investments that I have touched upon, I'm sure you're wondering about that old baseball signed by Mickey Mantle that your great-uncle left you in his will. This brings me to those other mysterious assets that people often talk about but don't really know how to evaluate. I'm talking about collectibles: art, antique cars, heirloom jewelry, antiquities, and sports memorabilia. Are they really investments? Yes and no. Do some well-preserved items from the past have value? Absolutely! Is it practical to dedicate a significant portion of your hard-earned money to buying up old stuff? Probably not.

I'm sure you can think of a few hurdles to investing profitably in antiques and collectibles. I will mention some of the inherent difficulties of capitalizing on the value of gifts of days gone by. All physical assets have variable value based on the following very important factors:

1. Authenticity
   You have to be able to prove the age and origin of the item, and you need someone or some organization to verify and certify authenticity for you.

2. Condition
   You have to maintain the item in pristine condition (usually) in order to find an interested buyer. If you can't sell it, it has no value.

3. Market
   You have to find either a market in which to sell the item or a private buyer. Again, if you can't sell it, it has no real value.

4. Age
   Some items become more valuable with age. The problem with that is you have to store the item, maintain it and wait precious time, sometimes long periods with uncertainty, to hopefully accumulate value.

5. Function
   With antique cars, toys, and mechanical objects in particular, but also sometimes with heirloom jewelry, the value of the item may depend on its functionality. Does it still work? Can it be used, worn, displayed, played with? The answers to these questions are important in determining the value of an antique or collectible.

Few people hit the jackpot with treasures found in Grandma's attic when they appear for evaluation on *Antiques Roadshow*. It's pure luck 99 percent of the time. Do some people make money from collecting old stuff? Sure. But such people make it a career choice and sometimes get their own show on the Discovery Channel. What I'm saying is, you need to be dedicated to the task. It requires a lot of upfront investment, takes up a significant amount of time to stay updated on market trends, and involves a good amount of risk. People are fickle, and demand for certain items can boom and bust with the wind.

My uncle, one of the twelve in my big Irish/Italian family, is incredible at building things. He has a passion for restoring antique cars. He is so good that he could have his own show, like *Overhaulin'* or something. I'm always amazed at what project he's gotten into whenever I visit. Back in early 2000, he got a deal on the chassis for a 1929 Peerless Roadster. It was one of three of that year's model in known existence. He set out to rebuild the whole thing. He procured parts from around the world and even fabricated some of his own parts to the exact specs of the original Roadster. By the time he had finished with the gorgeous car ten years later, he was more than one hundred thousand dollars deep into the project. When I asked him about what his plans were for the car in the future, he said he would eventually sell it, but that with all the money, sweat, and tears he put into it over the years, and given the rarity of this particular model, he expected no less than one million dollars for it. Of course, I gasped. My eyes widened and I wished him luck. Then I asked him for a ride. The car was in mint condition, simply flawless. I felt that I was experiencing the Roaring Twenties puttering along in that topless beauty.

My uncle kept it for six years—sheltered it, maintained it, polished it, and tuned it up. Of course, this care and storage cost him even more. When he finally decided to sell it, because he wanted to start another project and needed the space in his garage, he sold it at auction for barely fifty thousand dollars. Again, when he told me that, I gasped. Then my eyes widened and I wished him luck on his new project. You see, my uncle does this as a passion, a hobby. If he did it as an investment, then as his financial adviser, I would advise him against further projects. What my uncle experienced doesn't necessarily mean that the same will happen to you. However, I do caution anyone who is thinking about trying to make money in antiquities to be very serious about it, to be very well-connected to the marketplace in which the particular items trade, and to be mindful that it's no sure thing.

Complex Stuff You Hear about but Don't Really Understand (Also Known as Derivatives)

Talking heads on TV and industry publications such as the *Wall Street Journal* often talk about "hedging" types of investments in the marketplace. The average investor doesn't have a clue about **derivatives**, and oftentimes with good reason. Derivatives are just what they sound like in the simplest of terms—they are securities, or rights to securities, that are derived from other assets. They can be complex, risky, and terribly unpredictable. There are such things as stock derivatives, bond derivatives, commodities derivatives, and currency derivatives, to name a few. The most common types of derivatives that you've probably heard about are stock options, commodities futures, and currency futures.

Let's focus on stock options. You often run into the topic of stock options when discussing employee benefits or the compensation packages for CEO- or executive-level employees of publicly held companies. A stock option is the right to *buy* a particular stock or the right to *sell* a particular stock. The right to buy a particular stock is called a **call option**. The right to sell a particular stock is called a **put option**. In the financial media, they are referred to as **calls** and **puts** for short. Call options are typically used in compensation packages. The call option that an executive receives as part of his or her salary usually allows him or her to buy the stock at a certain price, normally reduced from the market value, as incentive. Many publicly traded companies allow their employees the right to buy the company stock at a reduced price as a benefit. At its essence, this benefit is a call option.

Puts and calls are also sold as securities in their own right on the open market. For example, if you were interested in a stock but weren't yet fully committed to buying it, you might want to hedge your bet on that particular stock by purchasing the right to buy that stock (a call option) at a price that you find attractive. The right to buy the stock (the call) would have a price, but it would be a fraction of the price of the actual stock. If the stock price were to go up after you purchased the call option, you would then realize a profit and would have the option to either purchase the stock at the option price (referred to as "exercising the call") or sell the option itself to someone else who is seeking to buy the underlying stock. If, however, the price of the underlying stock were to go down after you purchased the call, the option would be worthless because you would never pay more for a stock than the market dictates, nor would anyone else.

Let's look at a hypothetical example:

You would like to buy about fifty shares of Disney stock, and you see that the price has fluctuated over the last three months between $45 and $55 per share. You think Disney is a good value at $45, but you're not willing to pay the peak price of $55. You see (in the *Wall Street Journal* perhaps) that someone is selling fifty calls for Disney stock at $45 for $5 each. Your call options would expire in ninety days. You decide to purchase the calls and wait and see. You are comfortable watching the stock between now and then, and of course you hope the price goes way up.

How much have you spent so far? You have to include the price of the options in your total expenditure on the stock. That way you can evaluate your actual profit or loss when the time comes to sell the stock. So:

$$50 \text{ calls} \times \$5 = \$250$$

You watch the market over the next month and see that Disney stock goes from $45 to $47. You're pretty happy but decide to wait another month and see what happens. You really need to wait until the price is at least $50 to get your money back from the purchase of the options. You already spent $5 per share, and if you were to exercise the calls at $47, you will have only realized a gain of $2 per share, guaranteeing a loss of $3 per share from the get-go. Ultimately you would want the price to go much higher; as your profit increases, the higher the market price goes.

Let's look at two possible outcomes for this scenario:

Possible outcome #1—You wait sixty of the ninety days and see that the stock price for Disney has gone up to $55. You can cash in and sell the options to someone on the open market and realize an immediate gain depending on the price at which you agree to sell the options. The price would be somewhere between $5 and $10 because you wouldn't sell the options for less than you paid, and a buyer wouldn't necessarily buy them for the entire difference between the strike price and the current price of the stock shares unless he or she absolutely believed that the stock price was going to climb even higher. Or you can exercise the calls and buy fifty shares of the stock at your original preferred price of $45 ($45 × 50 = $2,250). If you decide to buy the stock, you have the option of selling it immediately for $55 per share (thereby realizing an immediate gain of $250: $55 × 50 = $2,750 − $2,250 + $250 [for the calls]) or holding onto it if you believe it will continue to go up. Either way, this is a favorable outcome.

Now let's look at the same simple example from the downside. Remember, derivatives are typically much more volatile than stock shares because they are completely based on speculation. You *think* a stock will move in a certain direction, and you buy an option to help you maximize that opinion. One never knows what will happen with the market.

Possible outcome #2—You wait and wait and wait, and the stock continues to drop in price, below $45 per share. Your ninety days come and go and your options expire. They were worthless. You lost your $250 outlay for the calls. This is a rudimentary example. It is less expensive to lose $250 in the short term than to have bought the stocks outright at $50 (50 × $50 each = $2,500) and then watch them lose value for an extended period of time. If you are a "buy and hold" investor, this may very well happen to you from time to time. However, if you're looking for short-term gains but aren't comfortable with a large outlay of cash, calls could come in handy. But you still lost $250 here.

Put options are the opposite of calls. They give you the right to sell stocks at a particular price. **Warrants** are rights to purchase stock at some point in the future. Now you're fundamentally familiar with derivatives. There are a few more of them out there, but these are the most common types.

I will throw out a word of caution here (in case you haven't already caught my drift): it is imperative that you understand the way derivatives work *before* you start speculating in them. Just as you would have a good understanding of a company's value, earning potential, and standing in the marketplace before purchasing its stock, you would need an ironclad argument for speculating the direction in which a stock will move before you start throwing your money around. Better to buy and hold one share than to try to get rich quick. That's all I'm going to say about that. Just a little mention to address that derivatives exist, but I do not believe that they are an appropriate investment vehicle for the average investor. That's not to say they are beyond comprehension. I believe they require a lot of research, attention, and understanding before they can be remotely valuable, and even then they are inherently risky securities.

Retirement Planning

This is my favorite part, and not surprisingly the longest part of *Money Moves*, as this is the area where I have spent the vast majority of my career in financial services. Retirement planning is a passion of mine and a vitally important aspect of American life. Yet, our country is headed straight for a retirement crisis with the continued withdrawal of seventy million baby boomers from the workforce. According to the Insured Retirement Institute, fewer than 26 percent of them are properly prepared.

Retirement is the single largest purchase you will ever make. It is essentially the equivalent of buying thirty years of freedom from work. That means it costs more than a home and a lot more than your kid's wedding (believe it or not) to retire. The current retirement system does not adequately prepare people for this major transition, and not because the tools aren't available. The basic practices required for sound money management haven't been taught adequately or with any sense of urgency. Many believe that Social Security will be their safety net, when in fact Social Security replaces only about 25 percent of a retiree's income, according to my experience. Could you afford a 75 percent pay cut and still live comfortably? You're not alone; not many of us could.

People may be inadequately prepared because we in the

United States have been transitioning from a time when people mainly depended on pension plans and Social Security to finance their retirement to a time when people have had to deal with the advent of 401(k)'s and reforms made to Medicare and Social Security that have made it difficult to pinpoint how much money will be enough to retire on. We have seen the systematic dismantling of corporate and governmental pension plans over the past several decades because the number of dollars needed to provide an adequate retirement living is so elusive and difficult to calculate on a grand scale, as is the burden of providing unknown lifetime income for pools of retired employees. That is why this burden has been shifted from employer to employee for most Americans.

It is with good reason that this transition is taking place. Americans are living longer, which is making the cost of continuous lifetime pension payments incalculable and unsustainable (not to mention risky to depend on). Just because there's a good reason doesn't mean it's not going to hurt a little. Not to be all doom and gloom here, but it's going to get worse before it gets better for the majority.

To compound the problem, many US workers are employed by small businesses and don't have ready access to employer-sponsored retirement plans. You might be surprised to learn that the average age when Americans start to think about saving for retirement is forty-four. What does this mean? In short, it means we're not prepared to retire on time. Because we are starting late, we are making it terribly difficult on ourselves to accumulate the sums of money necessary to replace our income when we stop working. It's a lot easier and less costly, with the tailwind of compound interest at our backs, to start saving and planning at eighteen or twenty rather than forty-four or forty-five. To wait that long is to have missed a whole lot of opportunity and a lot of money.

To illustrate my point, let's say you're eighteen and you just got a job that offers a 401(k) savings plan with your contributions to be deducted straight from your paycheck. If you were to start right then and there and invest $100 per month in a moderately balanced portfolio, never changing it throughout your entire career (an unlikely scenario, I know, but I'm trying to keep this simple), then you will have amassed $313,000 by the time you turn sixty-five. Alternatively, if you were to start saving for retirement at age forty-four in a similarly moderate portfolio, then in order to have $313,000 by age sixty-five, you'd have to invest $622 per month! That is the power of time and compounding interest at work!

So, what do we do about this? We do exactly what you're doing right now. We learn, we get educated about what to do, and we take immediate and meaningful action. We teach our kids to save and plan from the time they start their first job, and we help our friends and family learn this important information so that they can do the same for themselves. We perpetuate a new culture of preparedness and financial savvy so that future generations will make it second nature to save appropriately and have the power of choice over their lives and retirement. That way, our kids won't end up sandwiched like we are—taking care of their aging parents and their own kids at the same time because their parents didn't have any other options or income to support their independence.

The two biggest concerns for most people nearing retirement age are outliving their money and becoming a burden to their children. Retiring with independence and dignity is currently a privilege in our great country, when it should be a standard. That needs to change, and we can do something about it! Learning to drive is a standard for most people who grow up in the United States. At first it seems scary. You start when you're young and you have somewhere you want to go. Then you learn the necessities, and before you know it, it's just another habit; you barely need to think about it. Preparing for retirement is similar. It's a basic skill set - like personal hygiene or learning to drive.

It's just that people tend to get skittish when it comes to dealing with money.

All this talk is not meant to scare you. But the truth is serious, and you deserve the truth. I'm sure you're wondering how to get started and how to leverage your retirement benefits and options to help you become adequately prepared. There are quite a few options to choose from. We are going to take it one step at a time.

Before you decide which retirement strategy works best for you, you must make some peripheral decisions, such as how much money you will need and how and when will be the best time to finally retire. We will go through this decision-making process. But let's start with the most common retirement investment vehicles and work our way through to some that you may not have thought about but that are vitally important. Are you ready? I'm geeking out. Can't you tell?!

IRAs

What exactly is an IRA? IRA stands for **individual retirement account**, and you can get one at pretty much any bank, brokerage firm, financial advisory firm, insurance company and from most mutual fund companies. An IRA is really a title or designation that one applies to an investment account so that it will receive tax-favorable treatment either now or in the future. Think of it as a sticker that you put on an account that tells the IRS that you're trying to save for retirement and you'd appreciate a little tax help from them. You get to decide what you will invest your IRA money in by choosing your investment provider (be it your bank, a mutual fund, or some other financial firm account). Within that account you will have to elect investments that suit your financial objectives, that are appropriate for your risk tolerance, and that you believe will reasonably grow over time.

If your employer does not provide a retirement plan, then

yes, you should likely open an IRA. If you have access to an employer plan, you should participate in that plan first because employers usually offer additional benefits, such as a matching contribution, that are not available with IRAs. If you have exhausted your employer's retirement benefit and you want to save more, then an IRA might also be a good option.

There are two types of IRAs—traditional and Roth. Both have the same annual contribution limits, the same full retirement age, and similar rules for taking your money out when it's time to retire. But they differ when it comes to how and when you will pay taxes on the money, how much income you can make to open one, and certain other exceptions for withdrawal.

A **traditional IRA** is an individual retirement account into which you make contributions (or deposits) and for which you later receive a tax deduction when filing your annual tax forms. The deduction you will receive is equivalent to the total contributions you made throughout the year. There are limits set by the IRS as to how much you can contribute each year to an IRA. Since the money you contribute becomes pretax once you take a deduction on the contribution, the money grows tax-deferred until retirement. Once you reach the full retirement age for IRAs, which is currently fifty-nine and a half, you can withdraw money from the account at any time and in any amount. With a traditional IRA, what you withdraw is taxable income for the year in which you take the withdrawal. That is important because if you touch your IRA while you're still working, that amount is added to your salary to determine your total earnings. It could push you into a higher tax bracket and cause you to unnecessarily pay more tax overall. So be sure to carefully plan how much you will withdraw from a traditional IRA in any given year—it's counted as taxable income!

Before I go on, I must stress that retirement accounts should not be touched until you're ready to *retire*. That means either no longer working, working part time, working spare time, or working in a way that meets some other definition of being retired in some capacity. Retirement accounts are meant to provide tax-advantaged assets that will be used to replace income in your golden years. They're not suitable for short-term savings, taking a vacation, buying a car, or dipping into for any reason apart from retirement, really. I have a strong aversion to touching these accounts prior to retirement age to pay for college expenses for your children or grandchildren either. The penalties can be severe if you go in and touch the balance before normal retirement age. Your kids can get loans or scholarships, or (heaven forbid!) work to pay for college. You can't get a loan or scholarship for retirement.

A **Roth IRA** is a retirement savings account into which you contribute after-tax money (money on which income tax has already been paid). Because the contributions are made with money that has already been taxed (typically through your paycheck), you cannot take a deduction on the contributions for the current year. However, the money in a Roth IRA *grows* tax-free. Yes, I said tax-free. That means when you start to draw on the account at age fifty-nine and a half, the money is free and clear and you don't owe anybody anything more. You can withdraw as much as you like and the money is not taxable; you already paid taxes on the contributions! This type of account can be very beneficial for people in lower tax brackets and for those who have a long-term time horizon over which to invest (I'd say at least ten years so that the interest earned can grow to something significant that will justify paying the taxes on your contributions up front). Young people can take particular advantage of this unique type of account because they typically don't make more than the disqualifying income limit and they have tons of time to incubate the money and build up lots of compounding interest. When they get to retirement age, it would be pretty easy to have one million dollars in there to withdraw completely tax-free. Not bad for a simple habit as basic as getting dressed every day!

Let's take a look at one example of Roth versus traditional IRA savings:

Jane and Joe are both twenty years old. They both make $25,000 per year. Jane decides to open and fund a Roth IRA with $100 per month and invest it moderately. Joe decides he wants to open a traditional IRA with $100 per month and also invest it moderately. They both open and fund their accounts with automatic withdrawals from their respective checking accounts and forget about them for forty-five years (again, this is unlikely, but I'm attempting to keep this very simple). How much will they have and how will each be taxed by the time they reach retirement at sixty-five?

Well, $100 per month for forty-five years in a moderate portfolio will result in $275,599.61 in each account. So, they both have the same amount in their accounts, but remember, Jane already paid taxes on her contributions, so her entire account can be withdrawn without paying any additional tax. Joe, on the other hand, received tax deductions for his contributions for forty-five years, so although he was investing $100 per month, his tax relief each year made it feel as if he were investing more like $80 per month (on average). And in exchange for the more immediate tax relief every year in which he made contributions, the money that he was investing was considered before-tax money by the IRS. This means that both the contributions and the earnings would be taxed as income when withdrawn at retirement. When Joe goes to withdraw that money in retirement, he will have to pay taxes on whatever he withdraws at the tax rates that exist when he retires (which, as we all know, can change according to the tax plan of the government).

What does this really mean? It means that in today's dollars, if both Jane and Joe are sixty-five and they both decide to withdraw their entire account balances, Jane would get her full account balance and Joe would get about $220,479.41 after taxes were withheld. I need to note here that I am keeping this very simple and assuming that the tax rates don't change for these two over the forty-five years or that they don't make more money over their lifetimes of work. Both those assumptions are admittedly faulty, but I am only trying to illustrate the point. There is no wrong way to save, and the right vehicles are highly dependent on one's life situation when one is deciding to save or invest for retirement. As we all well know, life changes quickly and no one's situation stays the same for one's entire life. That's my disclaimer. The details can complicate things, but I want you to get the gist of what each account can provide. Alternatively, if you have a good amount of earned income and you're in a high tax bracket now, it may make more sense in the long run for you to save on a pretax basis while you're working and withdraw pretax dollars later at a lower bracket when you can control your income in retirement. There are also other factors like the impacts and taxability of your social security income when deciding in which type of IRA may be best to save.

There are a lot of tools you can employ when putting together your own retirement income plan. The first and most important step on that journey is deciding to save. The next important step is deciding how much, and revisiting this throughout your life to make sure you're keeping pace with what you will need at retirement.

The annual IRA contribution maximum in 2022 is $6,000, and once you are fifty or older, you can contribute an additional catch-up amount of $1,000, for a total of $7,000. However, to contribute to a Roth IRA, you must not make more than $144,000 annually for an individual or $214,000 for married joint tax filers. There are no income limits for contributing to a traditional IRA. However, if you make more than $78,000 as an individual or $129,000 jointly, the tax deduction benefits are no longer available to you. What does this mean? It means that before you start making a lot of money, you should use an IRA as a retirement investment vehicle for the tax advantages it provides. After you start making a lot of money, there are other attractive savings options for you.

An important note to consider: IRAs do not have loan

provisions, so you cannot borrow money from these accounts. You are restricted from withdrawing money from them prior to age fifty-nine and a half, with a few exceptions, as follows:

1. Death (in which case the IRA passes to your beneficiary)
2. Disability (as determined by Social Security)
3. Financial hardship, including—
   a. Purchase of primary residence
   b. Avoiding foreclosure or eviction
   c. Paying for college for you or your dependent (!)
   d. Death of an immediate family member
4. Rule 72(t) or substantially equal periodic payments— essentially annuitizing or creating an income stream from your account if you're retiring younger than age fifty-nine and a half.

If you decide to withdraw money from an IRA prior to age fifty-nine and a half, you will have to pay both a penalty and a tax even if you qualify for some exceptions. In the case of financial hardship exceptions, you will likely have to pay a penalty of 10 percent in addition to the taxes owed. You will also have to prove that you qualify for an exception. The financial institution will not just take your word for it. They are trying to protect you from making a poor financial decision without good reason. And so am I. You'd be surprised how many people I have encountered who want to dip into their retirement fund whenever they feel like it. It's not a savings account; it's a retirement fund. If you keep touching it, there won't be any money left in there by the time you get to retirement! I can't even begin to think about the lost interest and compounding. It's certainly not meant to be used as an emergency fund. Many people make this mistake, and it ends up costing them so much more in the long run.

These are the IRA basics. Be careful about where you get your IRA from. I don't think that banks, although convenient, are the best places to get an IRA account if you're really looking for growth. They are a great place to get started if you need to build up a nest egg in order to save up the minimum for a mutual fund. Banks will usually let you open and fund an IRA with as little as $25 a month. You open it there and put it in a safe, reliable investment account such as a CD or money market fund, and when you have the minimum saved up (usually $1,000, or $3,000 for high-quality mutual fund companies), you can transfer the IRA to a mutual fund account. Some of the largest and most reputable brokerage companies offer IRAs right through their websites. I encourage you to shop around and get to know any brokerage or mutual fund company with which you may be interested in investing your hard-earned money.

It's pretty simple to get started. You go to the mutual fund company's website, select "Open an IRA," fill out the form, and boom—you've got an IRA. You've got to decide how much you want to invest. I think that once you've met the minimum initial investment, a great practice is to set up an automatic monthly contribution directly from your bank account through an online transfer or ACH. Consider your finances and what you can afford just to get started. This is a huge step, and as I said before, it's the first big hurdle to setting yourself up for a great retirement—getting started! Make it your goal to save adequately for retirement. That can't happen all at once. It may be a shock to go from not saving at all to saving 10 percent to 15 percent of your income, so start small, but increase whenever you find you have a little wiggle room in your budget. Get used to saving and putting money away for your future self. I like to think of it as paying myself first—that always feels good. I promise you, you'll thank yourself tomorrow!

Employer Plans

Many people will first be exposed to retirement planning and savings tools through their employers. There are two main types of employer-sponsored retirement plans: **defined contribution retirement plans** and **defined benefit retirement plans**. You likely have heard the term *401(k)* before. A 401(k) is a type of defined contribution retirement plan. The amount that goes in is defined by your contribution, and the amount that comes out at retirement is dependent on the performance of the underlying investments that you've contributed to over the years.

Defined benefit retirement plans are what they sound like. The contributions are not defined, but the outcome, or benefit, is. These are basically **pension** plans, and more and more companies are moving away from them. But we still tend to see defined benefit plans within government service industries such as education and firefighting.

Let's look at a simple example of a typical pension plan. Suzanne has worked for Bahamas Memorial Hospital for thirty years and has a defined benefit pension plan. The plan benefits outline that for each year of service, once she has been at the hospital for at least six years, Suzanne will receive $100 per month. After thirty years of service, her defined benefit is $3,000 per month (30 × $100 = $3,000). The reason that Suzanne has to work at Bahamas Memorial longer than six years to receive any pension benefit is because of what the plan calls a "vesting" period. Vesting means that you have to work a set number of years for the employer before you are eligible to receive (or walk away with) any of the plan's benefits.

Let's dig a little deeper and go over some of the other plans you're likely to run into.

A **401(k) retirement savings plan** is a retirement program that may be offered by for-profit companies. Companies are not required to provide any type of retirement plan for their employees; however, to attract and retain the best and the brightest talent, they must stay competitive with their benefits packages. The term *401(k)* actually refers to the section of IRS code in which these types of retirement plans are discussed. A 401(k) plan is offered as an employee benefit according to the plan document that is established by the employer in accordance with the rules set out by the IRS code. Traditionally, 401(k) plans have been offered on a pretax basis (like health insurance premiums), so employees can contribute with pretax money and enjoy tax-deferred growth until retirement. At retirement, as early as age fifty-nine and a half, the individual may withdraw income from the plan and be taxed at normal income tax rates at that time.

Within the past ten years, **Roth 401(k)** plans have grown in popularity. A Roth 401(k) is like a traditional 401(k) in the sense that it is offered through an employer as an employee benefit. However, contributions are made after income taxes are paid and then grow tax-free. If an employee is interested in participating in his employer's Roth 401(k), he can make contributions after his income tax has been taken out from his check, but just as with a Roth IRA, once he reaches retirement, any withdrawals he makes from the Roth 401(k) will not be taxed and will not affect his income tax bracket. Another important thing to remember is that there are no income limits for contributing to a Roth 401(k), so this is an attractive plan for people who earn more than the income limit for a Roth IRA ($214,000 for joint filers as of 2022). Be sure to find out from your company if a Roth 401(k) is an option for you if this plan is of interest.

For nonprofit companies, school districts, hospitals, and charitable organizations, a **403(b) retirement savings plan**, sometimes referred to as a **tax-sheltered annuity (TSA)**, is often offered. These plans function much like a 401(k); however, there are subtle differences. One typical difference is that 403(b) plans (named by the section of IRS code that discusses nonprofit employer plans) have an "early retirement" clause stating that if an employee is able to retire after age fifty-five, he or she may have access to his or her 403(b) money without penalty once he or she is truly retired from the employer. This clause is meant to complement many pension plans that have early retirement or thirty-year full retirement rules. For instance, if a teacher had started teaching at age twenty-five, typically she would achieve full retirement through her teacher's retirement pension plan at age fifty-five. If she also has a 403(b) established, she would be able to access the money she had contributed and its earnings at the same time. If 403(b) rules were the same as 401(k) rules, that teacher would have to wait almost five years to be able to supplement her pension income with 403(b) distributions. This rule allows pension plan recipients to access 403(b) retirement savings plans simultaneously. Something very important to remember is that long-term health-care and income planning gets harder the younger you are when you retire. The ages of eligibility for Medicare and Social Security income are much higher than fifty-five. That is an important consideration to pay close attention to if you're planning to retire early. I mean, who doesn't want to retire early?

A **457 deferred compensation plan** is similar to a 401(k) in that money is contributed pre–income tax and taxes are paid when withdrawals are taken at retirement age. There are many types of 457 plans, but I'll only touch on the most common two types here. A 457(b) deferred compensation plan is typically provided by government agencies and nonprofit organizations, but for-profit companies can provide them too under special circumstances. A 457(f) deferred compensation plan is only available to higher-earning or highly compensated employees (referred to as HCEs) and is limited to nonprofit companies. It is sometimes referred to as a "top hat" plan because these plans allow highly compensated employees the opportunity to save for retirement on pace with what they will need when the normal 403(b) or 401(k) annual limits will not suffice. The 457 plans have unique rules for contribution and unique ages for eligible distributions. Employers can offer their employees Roth 403(b)'s and Roth 457's as well, although not all employers elect to offer all types of plans.

Though defined benefit plans, or pension funds, are quickly going the way of the dinosaurs, I'd like to spend a few moments discussing how these funds are managed since there are many still in existence. A pension plan is typically funded annually by an employer with the money being invested into what is called a "pension fund." The fund is managed by an investment firm that is hired by the employer and their appointed pension board. The pension fund is a pool of money from which employees receive benefits as they reach full retirement age (according to the plan). As more and more employees retire, more and more withdrawals are taken from the pool of funds. Although each employee gets a once-a-year statement telling them about their benefits, they don't actually have a physical individual account set up. They share in the pension pool as they retire, along with the other employees who meet the minimum service requirements.

Pensions are beautiful in theory, but because pension payments are guaranteed for the life of the employee, they are risky for all parties. With advancements in medical technology enabling people to live longer and longer, coupled with the unpredictability of long-term interest rates, it becomes increasingly difficult to adequately prepare to cover benefits for the remainder of an employee's life. Some pensions even allow for the continuation of payments to a spouse or beneficiary after the employee has passed away. If a company has not made the correct assumptions or saved the appropriate reserves for such periods of payments, they end up having to default on their promised benefits. Alternatively, they may have to adjust the benefit for new employees in order to deliver to current retirees in the plan. It can become quite a mess.

There are regulations that require minimum funding standards for pension plans, and there are laws that require mergers and acquisition transactions to honor preexisting pension plan arrangements. The Pension Protection Act of

2006 was enacted to protect employees from their employers' underfunding of plans and essentially leaving them high and dry. Not only does this legislation require pension plan entities to carry insurance to help guard against this, it also requires strict adherence to the rules.

Prior to this act, companies increasingly defaulted on their pension obligations. Can you imagine working for a company your whole life, and as you get ready to retire, the company gives you a gold watch, a pat on the back, and the great news "Sorry, we can't afford to pay your pension, but good luck and best wishes!"? What would you do? I know I would be terrified. But that is exactly what has happened to the employees of some well-known companies in the United States over the last forty years. It's also the main reason why pension plans are being traded out for defined contribution retirement plans.

I argue that if my company wishes to provide a retirement benefit, then they should give me the money up front and let me handle and monitor the account. I'll be responsible for making sure I have the income to retire. I'm not saying that some pension plans are not very well funded and very successful for their employees, but I am saying that perhaps because of the era in which I grew up, I want to have control over when and how I retire and do it on my own terms. I know that's not how most people feel. I also know that very few people feel confident enough with their own money-managing skills to be able to pull that off, but that, my dear reader, is the point of *Money Moves*— and you are well on your way to having that competence!

Please don't get me wrong. Pension plans have served many generations of Americans, my grandparents included, and continue to do so. With good reason, employees of many government agencies and most teachers still receive pensions. Teachers do not get paid enough to adequately save for their retirement, pay their living expenses, and outfit their classrooms for effective teaching and learning. But that is a topic for a whole other book! Private companies will always be the first group to determine the future of employee benefits because they must contend with competition in the marketplace and maintaining shareholder value. It is only a matter of time until pension plans become a thing of the past. Government agencies are slow to change, but eventually they do and will change. But everybody loves the idea of a pension nonetheless.

There are a few other types of employer-sponsored retirement plans that are less common but worth noting. **Thrift savings plans, cash balance plans,** and **tax-deferred annuity plans** are also offered as employee benefits, and these vehicles work in much the same manner as the plans just discussed. Each has its own particular rules for contribution and withdrawal, depending on how the employer designs the plan. With employer-sponsored retirement plans, the employers get to call the shots, choose their restrictions and requirements, and detail the plan rules as long as they are within IRS guidelines. There is no blanket rule for the options in the plan; one employer's 401(k)-like plan may have very different rules and restrictions from another.

"Annuity" Is Not a Four-Letter Word!

By now you've heard the term *annuity* a few times in *Money Moves.* Annuities have gotten a bad rap in the financial media over the past decade or so. I think that's a bit unfair, and I intend to make my case. The thing to remember about any financial instrument is that it serves a purpose, namely, to fill a specific financial need. Annuities are no exception. I think they are vastly misunderstood by the general public because they can have a lot of moving parts. I also believe that they will become an increasingly important part of a well-rounded long-term financial plan because of the guarantees they provide for lifetime income. It's important to note that there are no financial instruments that are suitable for every single person. Each individual has a unique experience, and someone else may need something much different from what you need to adequately plan a sound financial future.

An annuity, in its simplest form, is a contract between you and an insurance company that provides a guaranteed stream of income for a defined period, usually for the life of the annuitant (the person who will receive the payments). Because annuities offer some guarantees, they are considered insurance contracts. This is why they are provided by insurance companies.

There are two phases to the life of an annuity—accumulation and distribution. The accumulation phase of an annuity is the period in which money is put into the account to gain value. The accumulation phase lasts until the date at which the income payments are distributed. If you have a long accumulation period, the annuity is called a **deferred annuity**. If you turn on income almost immediately, you will have either a very short accumulation period or none at all, in the case of a lump-sum payment into the annuity instead of years of contributions or deposits. This is referred to as an **immediate annuity**.

The point of an annuity is to help someone protect or grow their investment and manage his or her income flow and longevity risk. Individuals may also have a tough time estimating how long their retirement funds will need to last, so an annuity can be used to help offset that risk. Annuities also can be used to manage lump-sum funds, such as payment from a lawsuit or an inheritance.

All annuities are meant to be retirement investment vehicles designed to provide income. These are long-term investments that have rules for withdrawal and guarantees for income in retirement. As with IRAs and 401(k)'s, the normal retirement age for annuities is fifty-nine and a half. I know this is a lot to take in, but don't worry, I'll explain.

There are two types of annuities with respect to the underlying investments —**fixed annuities** and **variable annuities**. Fixed annuities are not securities. They have stated fixed interest rates (like a savings account) that are guaranteed by the issuing insurance company. Fixed annuities are not invested in the market and are not regulated by FINRA (the financial services industry's regulatory body). They are provided by insurance companies and offer different interest rates and different crediting rate options for accumulation. They may have interest rates that are based on market performance, such as with **fixed indexed annuities**, but they are not actually invested in the market. The providing insurance company monitors the market and credits the interest rate to the policy depending on the crediting rate that the policyholder has chosen. There are usually three or four options for interest rate crediting.

These types of annuities can be a good option for those who are nervous about the market but want the opportunity for a better-than-average guaranteed interest rate. If the market goes down during the elected period, the annuity has a minimum stated rate of interest, typically 1 percent. This means that if you put money into a fixed indexed annuity and choose to have your interest rate determined by the performance of the stock market, but the stock market unexpectedly goes down, you will receive the minimum rate of interest. You will never lose money in a fixed annuity because of performance. There are, however, restrictions for withdrawal, and you could get back less than you put in if you take a withdrawal early and incur penalties. There are usually no explicit fees involved with fixed annuities as long as you leave your money in the account for the specified time period outlined in the contract and withdraw money according to the rules stated therein.

Variable annuities[7] have underlying investment subaccounts

---

[7] Variable Annuities are long-term investment products that offer a lifetime income stream, access to leading investment managers, options for guaranteed growth and income (available for an additional charge), tax-deferred growth, and death benefit protection for loved ones.

To decide if a variable annuity is right for you, consider that its value will fluctuate with the market; it is subject to investment risk and possible loss of prinicpal; it has various costs; and all guarantees, including those that are invested in the securities markets and are considered securities. They are also issued by insurance companies but are regulated by FINRA. These subaccounts function much like mutual funds but are enveloped within the variable annuity insurance contract. The subaccounts can range from very conservative money market accounts to very aggressive emerging markets or other sector accounts. These subaccounts are held in a separate account and not in the general account of the insurer. This means that they are not guaranteed to perform or provide a stated rate of return, and the accumulation of the account balance held in the separate account will depend on the performance of the underlying subaccounts. Many variable annuities offer both variable subaccounts and a fixed account option in the menu of available investment options. The fixed account in the annuity will have a stated rate of return or stated guaranteed minimum interest rate, or GMIR. Keep in mind that the fixed account assets are held in the general account of the insurer and are backed by the claims-paying ability of the insurer. This means that the funds are not FDIC insured. Insurance companies are not banks and are not regulated by the same bodies that banks are. Insurers are monitored for solvency, are rated for claims-paying ability, and have strict reserve requirements imposed by the government in exchange for the ability to sell products that provide guarantees.

You can find the prevailing ratings of insurance companies on any of the following websites:

- Moody's—www.moodys.com
- S&P—www.standardandpoors.com
- AM Best—www.AMbest.com
- Fitch Ratings—www.fitchratings.com.

for optional features, are subject to the claims-paying ability of the issuer. Limitations and conditions apply. There are fees and charges associated with investing in a variable annuity such as mortality and expense, administrative and advisory fees. Optional features are available for an additional cost.

The key thing to remember about annuities is that they are best used as a retirement vehicle to provide lifetime income. If income or legacy planning are not part of your financial goals, then an annuity is likely not the best option for your money. Because annuities have restrictions for withdrawal, rules about when you can access your account, and fees associated with the insurance guarantees, they are more expensive than traditional investment accounts. You may be asking yourself, "If they're more expensive, why would anyone want one?" Fees are an important factor to consider when comparing annuities to other investments. However, you can't compare an annuity's fees to a mutual fund's fees, because the two vehicles have totally different objectives. A mutual fund's objective is to grow your money. An annuity's primary objective is to help protect your money and provide and income stream in retirement. Yes, an annuity can provide growth, but that's not its primary objective. Mutual funds do not offer any guarantees. Annuities do. Remember that the guarantees are based upon the claims paying ability of the issuer. You have to pay for that kind of protection, just like you do with your car insurance. Essentially, an annuity ensures that your money won't run out before you expire. Why wouldn't you insure your money? We insure everything else in our lives against catastrophic loss, so why not our life savings?

You might have heard some of the popular financial commentators on TV trashing annuities as "very expensive" and "not worth it." My form of rebuttal is to ask a very important question: how can you guarantee that you will not run out of money before you die if you are among the vast majority of Americans who are not multimillionaires (as many of these people are)? It's easy to say that you don't need an annuity if you can comfortably live on a 4 percent distribution of your assets per year. Most people cannot live on a 4 percent distribution of their assets, which is the annual distribution amount recommended by most financial professionals that will give you a good shot at extending your money across your entire lifetime. The Federal

Reserve researched[8] to find that the average retirement account balance in the United States is $65,000 (in 2019). What's 4 percent of $65,000? That's $2,600 per year. *Per year!* Even if added to Social Security, that won't get you very far—it's a measly $216 extra per month. I know this is an extreme example, so let's look at someone who is in a better situation:

Suppose that Michael and his wife Janet have $500,000 between them in their 401(k) accounts. That seems like a pretty hefty sum for a couple of sixty-two-year-olds. Michael would like to retire now, whereas Janet thinks she should wait until their full Social Security retirement age of sixty-six. We'll talk a lot more about Social Security and the rules and penalties for taking it early, but for now, let's give Michael his way and Janet her way.

For the sake of simplicity, let's say the two of them have the same exact amount in each of their accounts and that they made the same amount of money throughout their careers. I know those assumptions are generally not true for everyone, but I'm trying to paint a picture here!

So, Michael retires at age sixty-two and takes his Social Security. To his surprise, his monthly check is only fifteen hundred dollars. He really wants to travel, and he starts planning vacations for each of Janet's time-off allowances throughout the year. Meanwhile, Janet makes about thirty-five hundred dollars per month. The couple is used to spending six thousand dollars per month on their expenses. They plan to keep their lifestyle the same in retirement as when Michael was working, but he is only bringing in fifteen hundred dollars per month with his early Social Security check. So, how much does Michael need to take out of his 401(k) to supplement his retirement income and make sure he and his wife can maintain their lifestyle? Do you think he might need more if he plans to travel?

Michael would have to withdraw $2,000 per month from his

---

[8] Federal Reserve Bulletin, September 2020 Vol. 106, No 5

401(k) to replace his working income. He may have to withdraw even more if he wants to pay for trips that they didn't typically take while they were working. The extra $2,000 per month comes out to $24,000 per year. He has $250,000 in his 401(k) account. Is $24,000 equal to 4 percent of his account?

Actually $24,000 is 9.6 percent of his total account balance. At that rate, without the travel, Michael would nearly be out of money in his 401(k) in thirteen and a half years, even while it was earning 4 percent interest every year. These types of excess distributions have a compounding effect on draining assets, especially if someone retires earlier. So, while Janet is trying to make her money last, Michael is running out of money by the time he turns seventy-six.

There are a lot of factors at play here. What if Michael's family members typically live into their mid-nineties? How do you think their budget might change as they get older and require more health care? What if something significant such as a disease or accident befalls them? What happens when they simply run out of money? An annuity could help mitigate these issues by protecting the couple's income in later years. It will not be easy to manage decreasing income and increasing health-care costs as time marches on. An annuity may fit into the overall financial plan to provide income for both the couple and legacy planning for their children in the future. After all, does anyone want to bet on a short life? I don't think so.

Now that I've got your gears turning about long-term financial planning, let's talk about a few of the most popular options that can be added to annuities (these options are called riders and they have additional costs) and some of the things to watch out for. Remember when I told you that retirement will be the biggest purchase you will make in your life? You're essentially buying thirty years of not working anymore. You're turning assets into an income stream for the rest of your life. These are very important things to consider, but sadly, most people spend more time each year planning their vacations than they do planning for their futures.

Old-fashioned annuities used to be "use it or lose it," just like car insurance. You would purchase an annuity with the anticipation that you would use it to finance your retirement, but if you died without using up all your money, the balance stayed with the insurance company. The insurance company would use the forfeited balance to cover those who conversely lived so long that they ran out of their own money and the insurance company had to continue to pay them until their deaths. In this scenario, the annuity really paid off! This sounds an awful lot like another very popular and old-fashioned retirement plan that people typically rave about but have no clue how they really work: pensions! Yes, consider an annuity to be like a personal pension plan that's tailored to your specific income needs and objectives in retirement and actually is your own individual account.

With any annuity, the individual investor is transferring the risk of running out of money in retirement to the insurance company in exchange for policy fees (or insurance premiums). This is still the case with modern-day annuities; however, insurance companies have recognized that people don't like the thought of dying young and losing their account balances to an insurance company. I can totally see their point, and the companies do too. That's why they have evolved the annuity to accommodate those concerns through policy riders. A rider is an optional feature for an additional cost that gives the policyholder certain access to the underlying account.

For example, if you are truly concerned that your account balance will not be used up during your retirement (that you'll die too young), you can request a rider that allows for the balance left over to be sent to a designated beneficiary. Some people will be more concerned that they won't have a large enough monthly income payment, so they elect for a rider that gives them a larger monthly payment. Some people want more control over the underlying investments in the account after they start receiving the income, while others want a longer period to be able to access (and perhaps withdraw) the money in their accounts after they start taking income. These are all possible rider options available in many annuity contracts. Some are more expensive than others, of course, but ultimately, most companies will custom-design an annuity to fit your financial needs and goals in retirement.

I will throw out a word of caution here: I never recommend that someone put all their assets into an annuity unless they truly have few or no other options. Just because you're in retirement does not mean that you don't need an emergency fund, and it should be something apart from your income source. I also firmly believe that although annuities can be an addition to a sound financial plan and can provide the kind of certainty that few other long-term investment accounts can, they still contain a degree of risk, whether they are fixed or variable, and those risks need to be carefully considered before investing any money.

You might be thinking, *What kinds of risks could be involved with a fixed annuity?* I'm so glad you asked! Just like any lower-risk investment with a fixed rate of interest, an annuity always carries the risk of inflation with the rising costs of living. If your investments don't keep pace with inflation, you are losing purchasing power and, therefore, money. Not physically, of course, but if you can't buy as much tomorrow with the same amount of money as today, then you are worse off financially. Alternatively, if you have a variable annuity and you've aggressively invested in some higher-risk subaccounts, your account value could actually decline. This can cause your accumulation value to go down and could affect your income payment once you enter the distribution phase.

You can lock in your monthly payment once you decide to take income. So, unless you have other assets, this will be a fixed income in most cases. Some annuities allow flexible payments depending on the performance of the underlying investments, but sometimes these can go down. Others guarantee inflation-adjusted income payments. There are a whole lot of annuity products offered by a slew of top-rated insurance companies. Be sure to discuss your needs, concerns, goals, and options with your trusted financial adviser before considering an annuity (or any other investment product, for that matter). Then, after you have decided on a course of action, be sure to compare fees, options, and restrictions before you decide which annuity may be the best fit for you. It's all customizable, and with the right financial partner, you can find something that will suit your needs perfectly.

I hope you understand a little more about annuities now. I also hope you can see that they're truly not a four-letter word. They are sophisticated financial instruments that serve a very real and important purpose in long-term financial planning. Think of them as insurance for your hard-earned life savings. No one wants to run out of money at ninety years old. You can make sure that doesn't happen to you.

Social Security

I put our discussion of Social Security in the chapter on retirement plans because it is the #1 most relied upon and most misunderstood retirement plan among Americans today. As long as you legally work for more than ten years (forty quarters) in the United States and have paid your FICA (Federal Insurance Contributions Act) taxes or you are (or were, in some cases) legally married to someone who did, you will be entitled to collect Social Security and Medicare once you reach the age of eligibility, which is sixty-two. I think much of the confusion surrounding Social Security is the reason many people jokingly refer to it as "Social Insecurity."

One reason for the confusion could be that people generally aren't taught how Social Security works, namely, how it is funded, when they can begin collecting, and whether or not it is a trustworthy system. To clear up this confusion, I am going to pose important questions for you to consider before you decide how Social Security will figure into your retirement landscape. Here are the top ten questions:

1. Who has to pay Social Security taxes?
2. How is your Social Security benefit calculated?
3. When can you begin taking your Social Security payments?
4. How much of your preretirement income will your Social Security payments likely replace?
5. When should you take Social Security?
6. How do your decisions regarding your Social Security affect your spouse and family?
7. What happens to your Social Security when you die?
8. Is anyone else able to collect Social Security based on your work record?
9. Do you have to pay taxes on your Social Security benefits?
10. Are there limits to the amount of Social Security taxes one must pay?

In addition to answering the foregoing questions, we'll discuss how sustainable the Social Security system is and what our government will have to examine in order to provide Social Security to Americans for generations to come. As the United States evolves, so too must our protective systems.

I'm super excited to discuss this with you (in case you can't tell) because I believe it is a very important part of your after-work finances. The topic of Social Security is not typically discussed between financial advisers and their clients because, frankly, there's not a whole lot of money in educating clients on a program that is provided by the government. I think that is a shortsighted view, though. Social Security discussions are vitally important to a solid financial foundation for long-term retirement and estate planning. Moreover, the decisions that Americans make about their Social Security income can have far-reaching and sometimes unintended consequences. The discussion itself builds immeasurable credibility and trust between adviser and client, which can only be an asset. It's important that Americans understand what they have, what their taxes pay for, and how to optimize Social Security, Medicare, and other state-provided programs to be better prepared for the rest of their lives. We are going to be retired for nearly as long as we were working (on average), so why wouldn't we want to be as prepared as possible? No good reason! So, let's begin!

1. Who has to pay Social Security taxes?

    Anyone who legally works in the United States, as well as the employers of such persons, must pay Social Security taxes. The Social Security tax rate for 2022 is 12.40 percent, half of which you pay and the other half of which your employer pays. If you are self-employed, you pay the entire amount. These taxes fund the OASDI Fund, or the Old Age, Survivors, and Disability Insurance trust fund. This fund provides insurance for when you retire, die prematurely, or become unable to work because of injury or illness. In order to be eligible for benefits from this fund, you need to pay the tax and work for at least forty quarters, or ten years, in the United States.

    Now you must be thinking, *Ten years doesn't sound like a whole lot of time to contribute in order to be eligible for retirement.* That is true. However, if you only work and contribute to the system for ten years, your benefit will be very small, and not enough to live on. We'll answer how the benefits are calculated and how to increase your benefits next.

2. How is your Social Security benefit calculated?

Each worker's Social Security benefit is determined by several factors, as follows:

a. how long he or she worked and paid taxes into the system;
b. how much he or she made while working;
c. when he or she decides to begin taking Social Security income;
d. whether or not he or she works while taking benefits (if prior to full retirement age); and
e. whether he or she worked for an organization that was exempt from paying Social Security taxes (not terribly common, but still relevant).

Your calculated benefit is not the same as the total amount you paid plus interest. Social Security taxes are invested in a trust of interest-earning treasury bonds, where they are kept separate from other federal money. When individuals retire, they draw on the trust, but there is no specific account for any one individual with his or her name on it. That's why you'll find some fine print on your Social Security statement that says something such as, "These are only estimates and may vary from the actual benefit you receive once you take Social Security income."

Of course, it follows that the longer you work, the more money you make. And the later you delay taking income payments, the bigger your Social Security benefit will be. According to the Social Security Administration (SSA)[9], your Social Security benefit is calculated by determining the average monthly income you earned over your thirty-five highest-earning years. A formula is then

[9] www.ssa.gov/benefits/ssi/

applied to the total, and a percentage of each bracket of the income (there are three brackets) is provided to the earner. So, for instance, you can expect to receive 90 percent of the first thousand dollars, 32 percent of the amount above one thousand dollars and below about fifty-six hundred dollars, and 15 percent of any amount over fifty-six hundred dollars. This process determines your primary insurance amount, or PIA, which is your estimated basic benefit amount. The Social Security Administration makes sure to remind us that the PIA is an estimate and urges us to speak with a Social Security representative if we have any questions.

The SSA claims that the benefit covers up to 40 percent of income for the average earner, but that hasn't been my experience. The average Social Security benefits that I have seen replace only about 22 percent of a worker's preretirement income. But I have predominantly worked with a segmented educated workforce primarily from health care and education. The percentage of income that Social Security replaces will be lower for those in higher income brackets. I have not met many people who can take an 80 percent (or even 60 percent) pay cut and still maintain their standard of living. This is why it is so important for people to learn about retirement planning early, to save often, and to begin thinking of Social Security as icing on the cake rather than the whole kit and caboodle. It will prove pretty difficult for people to retire solely on their Social Security benefits because of the high cost of living in this country. However, given that Social Security is a stable base of income that you can't outlive, it's important to know how your benefit is calculated and what you can expect from Social Security throughout your retirement years.

3. When can you begin taking your Social Security payments?

Your PIA, or primary insurance amount, is the monthly benefit that you will be eligible to receive at your FRA, or full retirement age. Your FRA depends on the year in which you were born. Take a look at the following chart to see full retirement ages by year of birth, based on the current law:

Year of birth	Age to receive full Social Security benefits
1943–54	66
1955	66 and 2 months
1956	66 and 4 months
1957	66 and 6 months
1958	66 and 8 months
1959	66 and 10 months
1960 and later	67

You may begin drawing your Social Security benefits as early as age sixty-two, however. This is referred to as "early retirement." Some people do this because sixty-two is closer to the qualifying age for other retirement investment vehicles. You can also delay your Social Security income until age seventy, at which time you must take it and can no longer defer. If you delay taking your benefits, you will get deferred payment credits. If you take Social Security early, your PIA will be reduced, like an early retirement penalty. For instance, those who take Social Security beginning at age sixty-two receive

72.5 percent of their PIA, not even a full three-quarters of their available benefit income. That sure saves the government a lot of money!

Many people ask me why anyone would want to delay taking their benefits. I bet you can guess at which age most Americans start taking their Social Security. You got it, sixty-two. The most common argument for taking Social Security is "I'm going to take it as soon as I can get it. You never know when you're going to die, and I want to be sure I at least get something." I can see where that argument might make sense initially, but statistically the odds are in your favor to live a lot longer than you may expect. Unless you know somehow that you will not live long enough to receive a substantial benefit from all your Social Security taxes, you should consider collecting more money in the long run by delaying taking your benefits.

Take a guess at the percentage of Americans who wait until age seventy to begin collecting Social Security. It's hard to believe that it's only about 2 percent! The best part about delaying your benefits is that your payments grow by 8 percent every year that you hold off past FRA. I don't know about you, but a guaranteed return of 8 percent year over year has been pretty tough to come by in the marketplace since the late 1980s. It might make sense to draw down some of your other retirement plans to allow you to delay Social Security and maximize the monthly payments that you'll never outlive, especially if you're in good health and longevity runs in your family. Just a thought. I would expect that as medical advancements continue to extend the average American life span and peoplecontinue to live longer, the FRA for Social Security will likewise go up, as has been the trend. I'm also sure that you've noticed that the normal retirement ages of all the different retirement plan options we've covered don't coincide with Social Security full retirement age. Curious, isn't it? Perhaps it is purposely built that way to encourage individuals to take control of their own retirement and have the option to retire earlier if they are able to save the money. I'm speculating, I know.

4. How much of your preretirement income will your Social Security payments likely replace?

    According to the SSA, Social Security replaces about 40 percent of the average American worker's preretirement income. Of course, the more you make during your working years, the less you will receive by percentage. In other words, if you were making more than two hundred thousand dollars a year, your Social Security would replace a much smaller percentage of that income based on the taxes you paid. Part of the reason is that the earnings on which you pay Social Security tax are capped at $147,000 in 2022.

5. When should you take Social Security?

    You should begin taking Social Security benefits when it is the optimal time for your particular situation. Things to consider include your health; your family history and genetics; your working capacity and earning potential; your assets; and other retirement income. In short, you should take it when you feel it is right and you have worked out the numbers in such a way to maximize your benefits according to your (and your spouse's) personal goals. Don't just take it because it's there. It may end up costing you a great deal, especially later in life, if you make a hasty decision without working out what each option means for you and your family's future income stream.

For example, if you are healthy, have longevity in your family, are able to continue working, and don't detest your job or don't necessarily need the income, you should likely delay taking benefits. Alternatively, if you experience unpredictable or unstable health, hate your job, are stressed beyond capacity, and would be able to live with your estimated benefit along with other retirement funds, then maybe you should take it early.

Another aspect to consider is that you have more options for continuing to work while also collecting benefits if you wait at least until your FRA. There is no earnings test for those who collect at or after FRA, which means you can work as much as you want and still receive your full Social Security benefit. But note that just because there is no earnings test, this does not mean your benefits won't be subject to taxes. If you continue to work and you make a substantial amount, your Social Security benefits could in fact become taxable. That's something to remember!

6. How do your decisions regarding Social Security affect your spouse and family?

If you are the higher earner in your marriage and have been historically, then your Social Security benefits may be dramatically larger than those of your spouse. The Social Security system allows one spouse to receive a benefit based on his or her spouse's earnings record. We all know that not so long ago, women were the predominant caretakers of children and often would take time out of the workforce to stay home and raise a family. If you have a ten-year gap in your highest thirty-five years of earnings, that can affect your PIA. A married couple has the option to examine each other's record and decide to take either their own benefit or half their spouse's benefit, whichever is larger. Additionally, upon the death of one of the spouses, the surviving spouse receives the highest earner's full benefit for the rest of his or her life. This is very important because if you collect your benefits at sixty-two and you are the higher earner, you could be penalizing your spouse for the rest of his or her life if you should pass away much earlier. Your spouse will only ever receive that reduced benefit, and it may not be enough for him or her to live on comfortably. As we age, it becomes increasingly difficult to manage a fixed budget with uncontrollable and rising health-care costs and living expenses.

I know I've got those gears turning up there in your head, but no, couples can't double-dip and defer their own benefits, collect on their spouse's benefit, and then switch back to their own at age seventy. Congress closed that loophole. Plus, you can't get both your own benefit and half your spouse's benefit. You can only ever get one or the other until one of you dies.

Upon the death of one spouse, the remaining spouse gets the benefit that was biggest, but only one—not both. I know this is a repeat of what I said earlier, but it's important to be clear. Lastly, you get one mulligan. If you decide to collect Social Security early and then within twelve months get a little more information and realize that you made the wrong decision, you can pay back the payments you received and defer your benefits until a later date. You have to do this within one year though, or your "get out of jail free" card expires.

7. What happens to your Social Security when you die?

    Social Security has a one-time death benefit of $255 for the surviving family of a deceased worker. As noted earlier, there are circumstances when your Social Security benefits can be collected by surviving family members. If you die with surviving young children while you are collecting Social Security, your children can continue to collect your benefit until they turn age eighteen. Your spouse may also collect survivor's benefits as early as age sixty based on your record without affecting his or her own Social Security benefits. He or she needs to be aware that survivor's benefits are subject to the earnings test (a formula that measures the amount he or she makes and the amount he or she would receive in Social Security benefits and adjusts them according to the limits set by the SSA) if he or she plans to work and collect. You must have been married for at least two years for your spouse to be eligible to receive survivor spousal benefits.

8. Is anyone else able to collect Social Security based on your work record?

    In addition to the spousal benefits that I mentioned earlier, if you have young children (under age eighteen, and nineteen in some cases) and are preparing to collect Social Security, your family may be eligible to receive benefits based on your record. There is a limit to the amount your dependents can receive, and between all of you, you cannot exceed the maximum family benefit, which is between 150 percent and 180 percent of your PIA. Let me give you an example:
        Larry and Gina are a married couple with twin boys age twelve. Larry just turned sixty-six, and Gina will be fifty this year. Larry decides to begin his Social Security

181

income at FRA, which is $2,000 per month. His total family benefit, according to his latest Social Security statement, is $3,600. That means that he can collect $2,000 for himself and the remainder of his family can collect $1,600 until the kids turn eighteen.[10]

There are some subtle nuances to the maximum family benefit rule, but you should know that it's available if this particular situation applies to you. I once had a client who was getting ready to retire and his children were still twelve and fourteen. He had no idea about this benefit and was still on the fence about retiring and collecting his Social Security. Once I explained that he was in fact eligible, and calculated the maximum family benefit they could receive, he decided to retire that year. He was happy, to say the least!

Your divorced spouse can also claim benefits based on your record as long as the marriage lasted longer than ten years. That means if you were married and your ex-spouse has a much better earnings record than you do, you could elect to collect based on his or her record instead of your own. If your former spouse is still living, you'll be limited to half his or her PIA. You don't have to even tell your ex-spouse that you're going to collect; you're just eligible as long as you can produce the legal documents to prove your marriage and divorce. Even more incredulous, you can collect survivor benefits if your ex dies and you were married longer than ten years. People anecdotally call this the "Johnny Carson rule" because Carson was married many times and a few of those marriages lasted longer than ten years! That means each of Johnny's ex-wives could collect full Social Security

---

[10] There are limits and rules for each person's share of the total family benefit. Kids and spouses have different limits depending on their ages, for example.

benefits based on Johnny's record without affecting each other's benefits. Yeah, I know I'm aging myself bringing up Johnny Carson, but still, isn't that crazy?!

I once had a woman in one of my Social Security seminars who couldn't believe it. She kept asking questions about divorced spouse benefits. Finally, after I had satisfied her by answering all her questions, she just smiled, closed her notebook, got up from the table, walked out, and retired the next day. True story!

9. Do you have to pay taxes on your Social Security benefits?

I have subtly alluded to this previously, but let's get into some specifics. If you have income in addition to your Social Security benefits, which most people will, there are limits to how much you can receive without affecting the taxability of your Social Security income.

According to the SSA, about 40 percent of people who get Social Security have to pay income taxes on their benefits. For example:

- If you file a federal tax return as an individual and your combined income[11] is between $25,000 and $34,000, you may have to pay taxes on up to 50 percent of your Social Security benefits. If your combined income is more than $34,000, then up to 85 percent of your Social Security benefits is subject to income tax.
- If you file a joint return, you may have to pay taxes on 50 percent of your benefits if you and your spouse have a combined income of between $32,000 and $44,000. If your combined income is more than

---

[11] On the 1040 tax return form, your combined income is the sum of your adjusted gross income, plus nontaxable interest, plus half your Social Security benefits.

$44,000, then up to 85 percent of your Social Security benefits is subject to income tax.

- If you're married and file a separate return, you'll probably pay taxes on your benefits.

At the end of each year, Social Security will mail you a Social Security Benefit Statement (Form SSA-1099) showing the amount of benefits you received. Use this statement when you complete your federal income tax return to find out if you must pay taxes on your benefits. Although you're not required to have Social Security withhold federal taxes, you may find it easier than paying quarterly estimated tax payments.

10. Are there limits to the amount of Social Security taxes one must pay?

There are! For 2022, you will pay Social Security taxes on maximum earnings of $147,000. That means that you pay taxes on all the money you earn up to that limit and that any earnings over that number are not taxed for Social Security benefits. One proposed reform to help further sustain the OASDI trust fund is to either raise or remove the income cap for Social Security taxes. It was raised in 2022 and will likely increase in future years, not only to reflect inflation, but also perhaps to help make the system more sustainable for future retirees.

Now you may feel a little overwhelmed about figuring out when to take Social Security, but you should be confident that you have the tools to make an educated decision. I can't tell you how few clients understand the consequences of taking benefits early or later or all the variables in between. Many people tell me they took Social Security early because they could but that they would have waited if they had known how to maximize their benefits. I have to rant a little here. There is not enough simple, clear and unbiased education on Social Security available for the average earner. People are confused about what their options are and many times make a hasty decision because they're presented with limited information. The Social Security Administration has a huge job to do. What I will tell you is that the representative in the Social Security office will not go through all your options with you. They will not detail what could happen if you choose a certain path over another. They will not illustrate what you might miss out on by collecting early or what you might gain by waiting a few years. They are there to help you do transactions and keep records. They are there to provide a valuable service, but do not rely on the SSA office person to tell you how to maximize your benefits, because ultimately, it's in the fund's best interest if you don't maximize your benefits. It's not purposely underhanded; it's just trying to get people the most money they could get today, but certainly not the most money they could get in total.

Rant over! Now you've taken the first step to making a great decision for yourself! Take a deep breath, smile, and pat yourself on the back.

I know I mentioned (rather tongue-in-cheek) that many people refer to Social Security as "Social Insecurity" because of all the press that the strained Social Security System seems to get in the political media. I mentioned also that the OASDI (Old Age, Survivors, and Disability Insurance trust) is a separate trust into which our FICA (a.k.a. Federal Insurance Contributions Act—our Social Security and Medicare) taxes are invested for future use. That's right, it's a separate trust into which our payroll taxes are placed for our future use. These funds are separate from the general budget of the federal government and should be treated as such. It is true that we have many more people who are living longer in retirement and are therefore increasing the demand on the trust. This means that the people paying in today are in large part paying for the retirees of today. It is estimated that the Social Security system as it stands today will be unable to pay benefits as currently projected by the year 2077. This does not mean that the system is bankrupt. It means that changes need to be made to address the longevity of the average retiree and the amount of promised benefits. According to Social Security Bulletin 70, no. 3 (2010),

> "Since the inception of the Social Security program in 1935, scheduled benefits have always been paid on a timely basis through a series of modifications in the law that will continue. Social Security provides a basic level of monthly income to workers and their families after the workers have reached old age, become disabled, or died."

This means, in short, that as the demographics and financial needs of retirees change, so too do the laws governing the level of income that is taxed, the amount of taxes that are levied, and the amount of promised benefits. There are many resolutions to the increasing demands on the OASDI trust, many of which have already been implemented since the earlier-mentioned publication, including increasing the age at which retirees can begin taking full benefits and increasing the cap on earnings subject to FICA (Medicare and Social Security) taxes, to name just a couple.

Now I must take a moment to congratulate you! You got through the Social Security section and you're still awake! Way to go!

Other Retirement Investments

We've discussed mutual funds, stocks, real estate, commercial assets, and insurance, but not in the context of using these vehicles to fund your retirement. They each have advantages and disadvantages in retirement. Some are highly taxable, some are unpredictable, some require maintenance, and others require a great deal of planning, backup planning, and nuanced strategy to adequately provide income for retirement.

It is certainly a sexy dream to imagine yourself living comfortably off a business that you grew from a start-up and passed on to your children, while you sit back and collect dividends. Or perhaps you have several rental properties that you've managed to pay off and you're thinking of living off the rental income. These are possibilities, but they require maintenance, and they're certainly not a guaranteed stream of steady income. There will be periods of drought in any business, including real estate. There will be hills and valleys with any investment. Unless you have a huge pool of assets that provide more than enough income for you to live on, where a 3 percent to 4 percent return would be plenty to maintain your lifestyle, you may find yourself having to shuffle money among a few different investments to hedge against temporary downturns in any one market segment or another.

Mutual funds do not provide a guaranteed or even a steady rate of return and are highly reactive to the market. Say you're retired and a market correction happens. You may need your mutual fund(s) to yield from 3 percent to 4 percent every year to contribute its/their share to your retirement income. What do you do when the market has a negative return and you're unable to take income for that period? What would be your backup plan?

Stocks would react in much the same way, but they have added nondiversified risks that affect the share price, such as management, industry trends, resource scarcity, product interdependencies, and the overall economy. Even preferred stocks, which typically provide dividends, may be unreliable if a company has a tough year.

Whole life insurance can be a great addition to the puzzle when you're using non-tax-advantaged vehicles to help fund your retirement. Whole life and universal life can build cash value within the policy that you can access tax-free in the form of a loan at any time. That cash value can help float you through down markets when other investments may not be performing so well. It could provide a bridge so that you wouldn't be forced to compound the effects of a down market by cashing out shares or making withdrawals on investments while they're declining in value. The cash value could buy you time to wait for the market to correct. You can use that cash value during your lifetime in the form of a loan against the policy. When you take the loan, you have the option to pay it back or not pay it back and have the balance be deducted later from the death benefit before going to your beneficiaries. These are just a few suggestions for building a solid income plan for retirement, but I'm not covering every base here, so be sure to discuss your needs at length with your financial adviser.

FUQYSBAs—Frequently Unanswered Questions You Should Be Asking

Now that I've walked you through the tricky but exciting waters of retirement planning, you should be asking yourself a number of questions that, more often than I'd like to see, are not even being considered. This is the point in *Money Moves* where you get to do a little soul-searching, a little self-assessment. I want you to consider all these things and really spend some time trying to answer the questions as best you can. You can revisit these anytime and check back in with yourself every year or two to see how much you've changed and how your priorities and strategies have evolved. Have your goals shifted? Are you even the same person?

Here they are:

- What does retirement mean to you? What does it look like? Visualize your future self. Close your eyes and really picture it. How can you prepare now to make that picture a reality?

- If you have a spouse or partner, what does retirement mean to him/her/them? Are your visions for retirement vastly different?
- What's your plan? Are you winging it?
- What does financial independence look like for you? How can you achieve it?
- How far along are you in the process right now? Are you behind, ahead, or on pace toward your goals?
- Are your goals realistic?
- Have you considered the costs of health care? What about long-term care?
- What do you want to do when you stop working? Will it generate income?
- What do you want your legacy to be?
- What are your priorities for your assets after you die?
- Are you protected against unexpected loss?
- Do you have people to take care of during your retirement? What about people who need to be taken care of after your death?

As you can see, there are a whole lot of options for investing for the long term, but gone are the days of sticking a wad of cash in a bank somewhere and living off the interest. What's important is that you think through the eventual contingencies and plan for these as you approach your goal of retiring on your own terms. You will never plan for every contingency, but you can give yourself a decent shot at protecting yourself against the most common among them. You can do it. You've just gotta plan for the worst and hope for the best, and you'll likely end up somewhere stuck in the middle with me! (Thank you, Steelers Wheel, for that awesome song!)

The Best Investments

When it comes to the best investments—a question I've been asked again and again over the course of my career—the pin always drops on the same spot. The answer is that it is a question only you can answer. Not to get all philosphical on you, but only you can know what is of greatest importance to you. Knowing yourself is the first step to making the best investments.

The old adage "Time is money" is useful when considering this question, but not for the reasons you may think. It's not that we should equal our time to units of value such as money, though in a very practical way that is a good idea. Rather, we should value our time to the utmost degree as though it were money— but of even greater value. Our time in this life is a commodity that can never be restored. It runs only in one direction for everyone who's ever experienced it, and therefore it is our most precious resource. Use it wisely. Be covetous of it! And be brave enough to admit what you really want to do and be in this life, because that is how you determine your personal values. That is how you decide what will make the best investments for *you*.

With that being said, I personally organize the best investments into the following three categories:

You: Health, Happiness, Quality
of Life, and Your Goals

You are the best investment you can possibly make. Investing in yourself is the surest way to improve your life. Your health, happiness, and quality of life are investments that will pay returns forever. And you'll never have buyer's remorse. I am not talking about temporary happiness. I am talking about enriching your life through pursuing education, passions, fitness, adventure, spirituality, and peace of mind. Each person's experience requires a different kind of personal investment. Sometimes the investment is simply a matter of establishing priorities. Sometimes it's an investment in organization, focus, and dedication. Sometimes it's a combination of time and money. Whatever you invest in yourself is worthwhile.

The saying I love most and use as my personal mantra is "You can't properly take care of anyone or anything else if you don't take care of yourself first." I don't know who originally said it, but I thank them through the cosmos for their wisdom.

Self-love, self-care, self-improvement, me time, Mommy or Daddy's time-out—whatever you want to call it, there are innumerable names for the practice of valuing yourself and your personal growth and well-being. You must be a developed and confident individual before you can be an effective asset to something greater than yourself, such as an ideal, or a company, or a family—the greater good.

Life is funny, and it passes us by quickly if we don't pay attention. Realizing it is a precious commodity, we must do our best to engage with and devour all that we are presented on this amazing journey. I don't want to proselytize, but I believe that money and well-being are not mutually exclusive. They are interrelated, and we shouldn't pretend that one has nothing to do with the other. When we have enough means to shift from survival mode to comfort mode, we are able to seek our own happiness, a true luxury. We should stop talking about money as if it's some dirty thing that virtuous people don't need. That's simply not true.

Do I think you need to be money-obsessed? No. Do I think it's healthy to be consumed with material possessions? No. Do I believe that the most rewarding and enlightening experiences you may have in life require some financing? Absolutely. If you're struggling to keep the lights on and put food on the table, you're not going to go back to school to improve your skill set, not backpacking through Europe, and not taking a month to meditate in an ashram in India. You're not even sitting on a beach at sunset with your toes in the water and your ass in the sand (thanks, Zac Brown), connecting with nature on the simplest level. That takes money. Prioritizing your well-being takes time and money and choice. Money affords you the ability to choose. Education, whether from school or experience, provides you with skills. Employing your skills effectively provides you with money. Your desire to grow, learn, and get better provides you with opportunity. It's a virtuous circle.

There are a lot of ways to invest in yourself, and some of them require no monetary investment at all. In fact, you can invest in yourself by cutting back your spending. Let's try an experiment. Sit down with a pen and paper. Archaic, I know, but bear with me. Make two columns on your paper. On the right side, print *Peace* at the top and list all the things that come immediately to mind that make you happy, content, relaxed and provide enjoyment in your life. Give yourself five minutes. Atop the other column, print *Stress* and list all the things in your life that make you angry, sad, confused, anxious, or upset. Give yourself another five minutes. The things you list do not have to be limited to what's immediately around you but can be anything that regularly comes in and out of your consciousness, things you spend time wrestling with even if only in your mind.

There may be words or ideas that end up on both lists because some things, such as money, spending, investments, projects, jobs, and children, can give us peace in our lives and also bring stress at times. That's okay.

Look at your lists. Which is longer? If you listed more stressors than peacemakers, then you know you have some decisions to make. It's okay to have stress in your life; in fact, some stress is good. No one has no stress whatsoever. If they did, they wouldn't have much in life that is important to them, or perhaps they would be the Buddha. The latter is unlikely though, right? Good stress keeps us active, growing, and trying new things. It can help keep us feeling young and motivated. There is a point at which good stress can become bad stress, though, and you have to keep that on your radar.

For example, say you volunteer at church and every year you head up the annual Fourth of July picnic committee. Everyone looks to you for leadership to make the event bigger and better than last year, but eventually, the pressure of coordinating a huge event and giving up your family time, especially on a summer holiday, just doesn't appeal to you any longer. You have to make a hard decision for your well-being. You're at a crossroads. You want to stay active in the community, but your heart just isn't beating for the monumental effort it takes to go big this year. What should you do? Is it better to give a half-hearted effort and do it begrudgingly or to share the leadership with others who might be more passionate and motivated this year? You have to prioritize and get your mind in the right place. Maybe you take on a contributor role instead of a leadership role, or you decide to sponsor in some way, or you bow out altogether, gracefully. Whatever you do, do it with everyone's best interests at heart and you won't make a wrong decision.

Back to the exercise. Look at the two lists you've made. Close your eyes and say this to yourself: "I cannot control the actions of others or forces beyond my own behavior and habits. I can only control how I personally react to those actions and forces."

Now open your eyes and go through your stress list. Cross off anything that is beyond your control. Of the things remaining, you probably can do something that will make you feel better about them. Even the smallest effort will make a difference. For instance, I put "planet/world" and "environment" on my stress list. I worry about how people treat each other, and I worry about how we all treat the environment. I can't control the planet or the environment at large, and I certainly can't control my neighbor's behavior, but I can change my habits to support sustainability and set an example of good environmental stewardship. That goes a long way, whether you know it or not. You'd be surprised by the influence you have on the people around you without your saying a word. They see you model certain behavior, and they are influenced in small ways. It all adds up. Actions speak louder than words. That is how being the change you wish to see in the world works!

I put "longevity" on my stress list too. How much control do I have over that other than making healthy lifestyle choices? My life span has more to do with genetics than anything else. So as long as I am taking care of myself here and now, how long I live will take care of itself. I can't control how long I will live. No one can. Cross it off!

Worry is a wasted emotion. Having stress because you are worried is something you can control completely. Rather than solving problems, worry exacerbates them, so it is better to eradicate it (or at least try)! The best thing you can do is to be prepared to take action when whatever it is comes at you, good or bad. If something on your list causes stress because of pure worry, cross it off. Make a practice of releasing the feeling itself. Sing the song to yourself: "Que será, será. Whatever will be, will be." It's stuck in your head now, isn't it? Preparation is the enemy of worry. No need to create problems where none exist. Remember that.

Now that you've cut items off your stress list, what does it look like? Is it a lot shorter? Good. No, great! Now you can ask yourself whether the remaining items are sources of good stress or bad stress. Are they manageable, or are they making you miserable? Is there anything that can be changed easily without uprooting your entire life? There are some things in life that will be stressful but the only solution to the stress is patience and time. A loved one's illness, a death in the family, a terrible job, and empty-nest syndrome are all huge sources of stress and aren't easily remedied in an instant. Bringing attention to the fact that it's a significant source of stress in your life helps you alleviate the tension. Even with big events or stressors in your life, you can find ways to ease the burden by adopting healthy coping habits. Meditation, exercise, alone time, spiritual guidance, and sleep are all great tools to help you cope. Managing the stress until it lightens is sometimes the best course of action. And be sure to maintain a lot of grace and patience with yourself. Sometimes the only way past the stress is through it. Embrace the suck and you'll get through it.

Money is a significant source of stress for most people. Money makes the world go 'round, yes, but it can also stop your world in its tracks. Money is a controllable source of stress. You either control your money or let it control you. I have said that money is necessary to live a good life and provide one with the luxury of choice. Those choices often determine how content one is with one's financial life and what role or power one allows money to play or have over one's well-being. You decide how big of a house you want. You decide what kind of car you will drive. You decide what kind of job you will accept. You decide what you are willing (or not willing) to do to advance your career. And through those choices, you decide what kind of lifestyle you will lead. You also decide how many kids you will have, where you will live, and what habits you'll have. You decide. I think the biggest money mistakes people make are made when they try to keep up with what society says is necessary to be seen as successful or when they acquire symbols of having made it. Ironically, those mistakes eventually make such people slaves to money. I call bullshit.

No one else pays your bills. Stop the nonsense. Cut back.

Live smaller. Give yourself the freedom to truly enjoy life, and make money the resource you'll use to build meaning and bring richness into your life. You don't need a two-carat diamond to prove that he loves you. Wouldn't a trip to Barbados be better (and cheaper!)? Find out at what point enough is enough for you. Take control of your choices before your choices take over your life. Do you really want to be married to a jumbo mortgage for thirty years, living from paycheck to paycheck? No. Get a more affordable house, or choose another location. Wouldn't it be great to have the cushion of an emergency fund or some extra savings in the bank so that when your boss has finally pushed you too far, you can tell her where to shove that miserable, thankless job of hers? Wouldn't it be great to do that thing you really want to do?

Look now at your peace list. Look at those things that make you happy, relaxed, and truly content. How many of them require money? I would guess that in some shape or form, most of them require a combination of time and money. Some are simple things that money can easily make possible, such as massage. I put massage and yoga on my peace list. Those require money. I try to get a massage once a month and go to yoga at least once a month, but I also do yoga daily at home. Massage ain't cheap. I know this, so I put aside some money every month to pay for my massages. It's also a flexible expense, so if things get out of whack for some reason in any given month, I can always skip it.

I took a yoga teacher training course in 2009 so that I could deepen my spiritual understanding of the practice and the philosophy behind it and also improve my form, both in body and soul. This was a significant investment of money and time. It was well worth it and provided me with a new set of marketable skills should I ever decide to teach, as well as a deeper understanding of my soul and my place in both the universe and the here and now. It spoke to me. I invested the money and became better for it. This was a worthwhile investment that has paid dividends for me in numerous ways. I am calmer and more present, and although it is a tough and constant practice, I am more mindful of my reactions to the world around me. This may not be the right solution for you, but I will tell you that anything that calls to your mind, body, and soul and makes you feel more connected to your miraculous life experience is truly the best kind of investment.

Invest more time, effort, and money into the things that bring joy, fulfillment, and peace to your life. Leave behind the things that cause more stress than they're worth. Investments in your joy help you navigate the residual stressors in life that you can't avoid. We have only one life. We need to live in the moment while taking the opportunity to prepare for tomorrow. It is a practice of balance. Leave worry and panic at the door, and welcome in planning, spontaneity, and flexibility. It may seem counterintuitive, but the balance between strategy and adaptability is really key to overall happiness. Be ready for whatever comes, and roll with it.

"So where do I put my money to provide me with choices? To invest in me? To make my life better, richer?" you might be asking. My answer will always be, "It depends." I try to get to know the person I'm advising so that I can give the most appropriate options. There is no "one size fits all" when it comes to financial planning. Each individual has different needs and priorities. Those can be determined by many different characteristics such as the person's upbringing, religion, or passion, but most of all the right answers are determined by the person's life experience. The most beneficial investments in which to put your hard-earned money will vary based on your values. So, I ask you, what is most important to you?

Do you hate your job? Become a better employee, go back to school, ask for a transfer, or start looking for something else. Most companies value good employees. The best employees can write their own tickets. If none of those work out for you, downsize and start over. Don't be afraid to take a step backward in order to open up your realm of possibilities for the future. The idea that life or careers only move in one direction is a fallacy anyway. Establish multiple income streams. Take a chance! You're never too old, too far along, or too anything to start a new path to happiness. If you're not happy, take baby steps every day to get closer to something that will make you happy. Just be open to possibilities, and be resourceful enough to seek out alternatives. You should also be willing to ask for help when you need it from trusted confidants. People want to help. Your true friends want to see you happy. Hey, maybe you'll write a book in your forties and try to help people better understand money. Who knows?! (wink,wink!)

Do you want to travel? Write down your top five travel destinations. Which are the most affordable? Research how much the trip would reasonably cost. Search your budget for discretionary money you may have each month. If you do have discretionary funds, allocate some of them to a travel savings account, and be diligent. Commit to a certain savings goal every single month. If you don't have any discretionary funds left over, go back through your budget and see where you could prioritize and cut. Perhaps you need to take your lunch to work every day. Perhaps you can skip the convenience stores when you fill up for gas. Maybe you can host a happy hour at your place instead of going out on Friday night. You get to choose. Whatever it is, you can find a small amount to channel in the direction of your priority. Figure out that amount and give yourself a time line for travel to this first destination. Save, save, save, and then enjoy your trip!

These are just some examples of typical ideas that my clients mention. The stressors are all too common. In general, people just want to be financially free. The first step to becoming financially free is to define what that means to you. What are your priorities? What is nonnegotiable? Is it really nonnegotiable, or do you need to have your perception turned on its head? If you look at life from a different angle and start really asking yourself the hard questions about what makes you happy or what makes you miserable, you might be surprised to find out the answers that you have been hiding from yourself for years.

I have had (and you have too) friends and clients who hate to clean and do chores, and yet they maintain huge homes with lots of toys. Guess what? Those homes and toys, along with all the furnishings and accessories that go with them, require maintenance. The more you have, the more it costs to maintain. You either do the maintenance yourself or pay someone to do it for you. Those costs add up. Wouldn't you rather have a reasonably comfortable house with little upkeep, a toy or two that you love, and very low maintenance costs? Pocket that extra money and go explore! Make yourself happy and unburden yourself from all that fancy stuff! It weighs you down. Trust me.

Find your enough. Don't buy a house bigger than you need. Don't buy more cars than you need. Don't fall into the trap of accumulating material things that you ultimately have to maintain, repair, and eventually divest. Your kids or other family members will one day inherit your stuff and will not have the same interests as you and likely won't care the same way you do about it. Estate and legacy planning are very important, especially if you do a great job with your finances in this lifetime. I can't tell you how many horror stories I have witnessed play out over the years of disorganized estates and lost money that has torn families apart. Estate planning is an important piece of your financial wellness to keep in mind in order to avoid a mess after you're gone, even if you don't have much. You'd be surprised.

Appreciable Assets

I defined an asset earlier as anything you purchase that you expect to increase in value. Therefore, an asset is appreciable. Your home, business, securities, precious metals and stones, collectibles, art, and antiques are all tangible assets that you can see and feel, and watch their values increase over time. Of course, you know by now that what determines the return on each of those investments depends on the market, the time period for which you hold the asset, and when you decide to sell it.

But have you considered other appreciable assets? Intangible ideas into which you put a good amount of time, effort, and yes, sometimes money don't always have a numerical value in the end but can bring value to your life and your happiness. I am talking about going back to school to increase your education and become more competent in a field of study that may one day get you a better job or a more suitable career. I am talking about taking an adventure to hike the Appalachian Trail and finding yourself in the process. You may consider making memories with your family, your friends, and your loved ones' appreciable assets, even though you may not be able to put a price tag on them. Education and experiences can be some hefty investments of your time, money, and commitment, but they are certainly worth it.

When I say appreciable assets, I don't just mean investing large sums of money, or a great deal of effort or time, all at once and then being done with the investment. I also mean the little consistent investments over time that pay dividends with continued commitment. Spending your time researching how your anatomy reacts to certain foods and environments is a worthwhile investment that can extend your longevity. Spending your money on a gym membership or fitness classes or equipment that enables you to take care of your mind, body, and soul will also pay off in the long run, but this may require small, healthy investments over time, sometimes for the rest of your life. Investing in the right types of foods, watching what you eat, and being careful about the fuel that you give your amazing body will benefit you in ways well beyond improving your looks. It will help you feel good, think clearly, regulate your mood, and attain peak performance levels. Those kinds of investments pay off now *and* later because you won't spend all your time and money in the doctor's office. Also consider the savings you enjoy when you invest in whole foods and vegetables instead of processed junk. Maybe you even have a vegetable garden. When you eat right, you give yourself the gift of health and wellness. As Hippocrates wrote, "Let thy food be thy medicine and thy medicine be thy food."

You may also find fulfillment by investing in environmental or philanthropic causes. These are wonderful investments that pay returns in the form of karma. Universally speaking, the more you give, the more you receive. The returns may not be specifically monetary, although you can save on your taxes with charitable spending, but they do hold a different kind of value. When you spend time and money on what enriches your soul, makes you feel good, and makes you a better human, you become a better human, and all of humankind is elevated.

Investments you make in the health of the planet are also appreciable. We don't have a backup planet. Learning to consume and live on less, and to reuse and recycle the resources we already have, allows us to continue enjoying this incredible life now and in the future. We need water to survive, but our water is polluted. We need to fix this. If everyone does their part, however small, that type of investment will sustain humankind for millennia to come.

Volunteering your time is one of the most expensive investments you can make and often the most valuable. When you give someone else the gift of your time, you are investing in their success. I have said that time is a finite asset; you can't increase the amount you get necessarily, but you can increase the quality of the time you have. By donating or investing your time, you are encouraging others with your example and are becoming a better, more empathetic human. The more empathetic we are toward our fellow beings and the more we understand their unique situations, the stronger we become as a global community. We can achieve peace if we understand each other and empathize with the experiences of people different from us. How do you learn anything from the people you hang out with if they are all just like you? You don't. You deeply ingrain narrow belief systems and view life from only one perspective. We must reach out and try to understand the experiences of other people around the world and, heck, in our own neighborhoods. We must work together to understand that all people really want is safety, love, and freedom. Those are three basic needs that fortunately, in the United States, we have been afforded through the Constitution. At least that is what is written in the law, but even in this country we have groups of people who struggle to feel free and safe and loved. If we consider ourselves an advanced civilization, we must include all our people in that protection. We must do better to set an example for the rest of the world and show that peace and freedom is possible for all people. Peace is the biggest payoff we could imagine for any investment.

Another set of appreciable assets is our mistakes and failures. Yes, you read that right. Our failures are valuable investments. Sometimes they cost a little and sometimes they cost a lot, but with each one we derive value. We learn lessons that help us grow and be more successful in the future. Every experience is an investment, good or bad. You are learning and getting better as long as you're paying attention and as long as you don't give up. The investment involved in a mistake or failure is only wasted if you don't learn anything from it.

Community, environment, relationships, family, adventures, new experiences, education, knowledge, wisdom, inner peace, spirituality, becoming better—a better person, sister, friend, parent, child, worker, leader, volunteer … you name it. If you invest all your assets wisely, you'll see positive returns. Life just gets better.

Sound Peace of Mind

There is something to be said about peace of mind. Your peace of mind is as important as showing positive returns. You've probably heard the cliché "Even a blind squirrel finds a nut once in a while." There are many types of investments, and most of them will show positive returns at some point in their life spans. That doesn't mean that every investment is right for you.

Many clients have asked me, "Should I pay off my house or keep my mortgage for the tax deduction?" As with most financial questions, the correct answer is "it depends." It depends wholly on your goals, your tax situation, your priorities, and what gives you peace of mind. If you're trying to retire early and your only major monthly expense is your mortgage, and if you have the money to pay it off, then you might feel more secure paying it off and decreasing your monthly expense budget. If you have a sum of money sitting in a savings account earning 0.05 percent and your mortgage is costing you 5 percent each year, you might want to pay it off. You might like the idea of not owing anyone else any money. Those are all completely valid reasons to pay off your mortgage. Perhaps you have no other tax deductions and your income puts you in the highest tax bracket without the mortgage. In such a case, you may want to keep your mortgage and its tax deduction.

That is just one example of a question that comes up frequently that has no definitive right or wrong answer. There are pros and cons to the many options available. Do what makes you feel best. In some respects, yes, you have to follow your gut. What you do with your money has to make sense to you and put your mind at ease. Invest only in what you reasonably understand. If you understand how something works and how it should make money, particularly when it comes to companies and how they profit, the quality of their products, and how they treat their customers and employees, then invest. Don't make guesses when it comes to your money; that's speculation and gambling. Stick to what you know. Do what feels good and right. Get yourself a coach. Anything in life worth doing is difficult, but because it is difficult, it is so much more rewarding.

Success, adventure, and fulfillment are all part of life's journey. Your life is a precious moment in time, a unique opportunity to glimpse the divine continuum of the universe if you see it for what it truly is. It can be difficult to stop and just be when one is constantly struggling to survive. It is only when one has the luxury of comfort and stability, as in a roof over one's head, clean water and air, heat in the wintertime, and food on the table each night, that one can begin to explore the wonder of life. When one is not struggling to make ends meet, one has the luxury of time, the most precious currency of all.

Let's do another exercise. You're going to make a vision board. It can be as simple as a piece of poster board with magazine cutouts and drawn pictures, along with words and phrases in magic marker. If you want to get fancy, type "vision board kit" into Amazon or Google and buy one. Jack Canfield makes one that is nice. A vision board can help you visualize your goals, financial or otherwise, every day. You will draw and paste pictures of your goals and aspirations, and write words and quotations that inspire you, all over your board. The activity gets you thinking about what you want to do and where you want to be in life. A group of pictures that you can easily see each day helps program your subconscious to take small steps regularly toward what you want. You can put anything on the vision board; it's only for you. When you are done, make sure it is hung or displayed someplace you can see it every day.

How does this exercise clue you in to what really gives you peace of mind? Use your board as a guide when considering your investment options.

Another great tool that I use is my annual personal and professional goal lists. I take a simple piece of paper and write the year in big numbers at the top. On the right side, I write "Professional," and on the left, I write "Personal." Then I draw a line down the middle of the page. I write down my personal and professional goals in relatively big letters and in bullet format, each in a few simple words. I try to limit my goals to five or six for each column (or less). When I try to do too much, I end up getting nothing done, so I try to keep it big-picture for the next year. I tape it up in my office right next to my computer so I know that I will see it very often, if not every day. I glance at it as a reminder to keep myself on track and have the goals in the back of my mind. As I work toward the goals throughout the year, I cross each one off as it is accomplished, one by one and not necessarily in order. At the end of the year, usually after Christmas but before New Year's Day, I look over my list to see what I did and didn't get done. Some goals will roll over to the next year; some I will reevaluate. Some are big and some are small, but I always go through this ritual sometime around December 31 to get myself energized and focused on the year to come.

If you want to be successful, financially free, and comfortable in your life, you have to work for it. Set yourself up for success by getting organized. You will succeed if you have a plan and you work it. There is no right way to make money. You have to do what is right for you. Provide yourself a solid foundation and invest your precious time, money, and effort into the things that interest you most—and that is all.

EPILOGUE

The Bottom Line

If you have skipped to the back pages for the spoiler at the end just to get the gist of *Money Moves*, I have good news for you! I'm going to tell you the main theme, the whole shebang, the point. If you get nothing else out of this whole book, then take *this* with you: *live within your means*; trust in your ability to learn about, grow, and handle your own money; save as much as you can when you can; and invest in yourself always. Try to be better tomorrow than you are today, if by only a fraction of a percent, but better nonetheless. You will gain wealth, you will be successful, and you will achieve your goals and dreams. Just don't give up!

ACKNOWLEDGEMENTS

First and foremost, I have to thank my ride-or-die, Jeremy. We marvel at the good fortune in our lives often and wonder how a couple of crazy college kids managed to make it 25 years and still want to be with each other more every day, but here we are. Just so damned lucky. Thank you for believing in me and all my crazy ideas, without fail. It means the world.

Mom, you are the reason I am who I am. Period. Thanks. You did an awesome job! :P

Caitlin and Lola, you're my why for everything. I have to thank you for keeping me motivated. You light up my life.

To all the incredibly strong women in my life that inspire me to lead, be loud, have opinions and believe that my experience and knowledge mean something to the world. I have been incredibly blessed to be surrounded by female role models who know how to use their voices without apology. It's awe-inspiring. If we're friends or family, that means you. Thank you.

Finally, to Garry and Tamara who called me out and got me to stop talking about writing a book and actually start writing one. Thank you for believing that I could achieve this dream. The day we did the reciprocity circle was a significant turning point. I will never forget it.

APPENDIX A: SOURCES OF STATS

Chapter 1, Page 18
American Psychological Association, *Stress in America*, 2016, http://ar2016.apa.org/stress-in-america/.

Chapter 3, Page 63
S.Kumar, "3 Reasons the average American may be worse off than Greece", *Fortune*, July 9, 2015.

Chapter 7, Page 148
What was the Average Annual Salary in the U.S. in 1950? www.reference.com/business-finance/average-annual-salary-u-s-1950-76b0654d84ee2912

Chapter 7, Page 149
https://www.census.gov/acs/www/data/data-tables-and-tools/narrative-profiles/ "American Community Survey, Household Income in the United States in 2015-2019

https://www.statista.com/statistics/240991/average-sales-prices-of-new-homes-sold-in-the-us/"Average sales price of new homes sold in US from 1965 to 2021"

Chapter 8, Page 174
Arslan, Kristie. "Five Big Myths About American Small Businesses", *Huffington Post*, May 24, 2011.

Chapter 9, Page 208
Federal Reserve Bulletin, September 2020 Vol. 106, No 5

Chapter 9, Page 217
www.ssa.gov/benefits/ssi/

APPENDIX B:
INTERVIEW QUESTIONS FOR POTENTIAL ADVISERS

1. How long have you been in the financial services industry? Or how long have you been doing this? This establishes experience and some credibility, if they are still in the industry and haven't had their licenses revoked, that's a good thing. You can check on the status of licensure at www.brokercheck.com.

2. What types of services do you provide? Do you have a specialization? Is there anything you can't do? (ie: give advice, sell insurance, estate planning, etc.)

3. What types of fees are associated with the products that you are selling (to me)? How do you get paid? (Fees are not the end-all, be-all, but they are important. You need to know what you're paying for and if you feel it is worth it. If an adviser is hesitant to disclose fees or doesn't feel confident that their product solution justifies the cost, there is a disconnect. If they do not disclose fees or say "there are no fees," be wary. Very few investments, save some fixed-interest vehicles, are fee-free. No one manages investments or securities for free.)

4. Can you provide me with an estimate of what I should reasonably expect to have if I follow your recommendation or advice?

5. Can you provide me with a strategic roadmap to help me achieve my goals, step-by-step? How often will you check in with me to make sure we're on track?

6. Can you detail my responsibility in this partnership so that I know what to expect from you and what I am expected to do? (Yes, you have to work at this too. It's a partnership, not a solo mission. You and your adviser have to work together to achieve YOUR goals. After all, they are yours and it's your money! It's in your best interest to be personally involved. It leads to better outcomes too because you know what's happening and what's expected every step of the way.)

7. Is it possible for me to achieve my goals or are my expectations unreasonable? (If your adviser can't be straight with you and tell you the truth when you're being totally unreasonable, you may want to keep looking. You need a coach, and sometimes coaches need to get real. You don't need a yes man.)

8. What are the pros and cons of the products/investments that you are recommending to me? (You need to know the good, the bad, and the ugly. If an adviser only tells you wonderful, great, exhilarating things about the investment proposal and does not mention the risks, fees, and trade-offs you should be skeptical.)

9. What qualifications do you have? What field of study brought you to your career? (It's important to know that your adviser is knowledgeable and competent on the subject matter. Insurance and securities regulations change constantly and your adviser needs to stay abreast of changes in the industry, how it is regulated, and ultimately affected by outside factors including but not limited to, the economy, the market, inflation, interest rates, government actions, and all sorts of other important money-related stuff. They won't have a crystal ball, no one does, but they can help you understand what the

market does, what it will do and how your investments will react to those changes.)

10. What do you love about your job? Money is a deeply personal part of life and it's important to know your adviser's motivation. It's also important to get to know them as a person if you're going to trust them with the most intimate details of your financial life. This is a partnership and partners need to know each other authentically.

I can be reached on twitter: @MoneyTree78;
Instagram: @TreefromMoneyMoves
Facebook: Theresa Garvin Yong

Printed in the United States
by Baker & Taylor Publisher Services